# Curiosity

## ~~Killed~~ made the Cat
### made

Breaking the Rules and
Becoming Extraordinary

# Curiosity

## ~~Killed~~ the Cat
### *made*

Breaking the Rules and
Becoming Extraordinary

## J. LARRY STEVENS

BLACK VEIL PRESS

No part of this publication may be reproduced, stored in a retrieval system, or transmitted, in any form by any means, electronic, mechanical, photocopying, recording, or otherwise, without prior written permission from the publisher.

2017 Black Veil Press, LLC

197 65th Terrace North, West Palm Beach, FL 33413
www.blackveilpress.com

ISBN: 978–0–9883885-2-9

Printed and bound in the United States of America

First Edition

# Table of Contents

Also by J. Larry Stevens

*Riding Elevators Backwards*

# Author's Note

First and foremost, this is a story about the journey from Average to Extraordinary. It is my story now, but I want it to become your story. It is not a fairy tale, and the journey is not a mythical or metaphorical one. It is real, and regardless of your business or profession, you are already a fellow traveler. The journey from Average to Extraordinary is long and winding with great expanses of straight roads and beguiling sunshine, interrupted more often than not by treacherous turns, threatening storms, and pounding headwinds. The trip is not for the faint of heart, and some people never leave the comfort of their current surroundings to begin the adventure. Many who do are thwarted by washed out roads and broken bridges; others make wrong turns and are never able to find their true north; and still others travel well, surviving hailstorms and lightning strikes, only to give up in the face of ceaseless winds of discouragement and criticism. But those who stay the course, navigate the obstacles, and, in the words of Winston Churchill, "never, never, never give up," are rewarded with an extraordinary adventure. So get prepared; you are in the driver's seat. Follow the map and watch for signs. Extraordinary is just ahead!

# Acknowledgments

Thanks to the five women in my life: Lynn Stevens, servant leader, caring lawyer, and guiding beacon for fifty years—she remains my only light; my grandmother whose inimitable spirit of encouragement laid the foundation; my mother whose moral fiber grounded me ethically; Keri Lynn Lurtz, daughter and creative muse who is not afraid to break the rules, drove this book and is responsible for any creativity it possesses; twin granddaughters, Alexandra and Isabella whose boundless joy always fascinates and enthralls.

To son Jay Stevens, blockchain and cryptocurrency guru; the kid chasing butterflies in right field who never lost that curious spirit for the unexplored. To grandson James, my aspiring chef, who proves the thesis of this book with his ability to take the ordinary and create the extravagant. And grandson Garrett, the real writer in the family who taught me the discipline of writing every day and the importance and power of Story.

To Dr. Mike Salvador who did a first read and provided invaluable insights, Martin Wade who taught me most of what I know about mergers and acquisitions, Dr. Tim Mescon who was the first to encourage me to teach and paid me to do it, and David Ledbetter who on my first assignment with Price Waterhouse spent three patient hours teaching me to write a one-page memo. Dave, a thank you that is forty years late.

**JLS**

# Introduction

Historians will one day look back and note that the beginning of the 21st century was the start of America's decline into the inescapable depths of mediocrity. This is not to suggest that America will no longer be competitive in the global marketplace, or the democracy we love will fall prey to socialistic or other forms of government and lose its place on the world stage. Rather, the year 2000, which started with such exuberance for the individual spirit and hope for the future, will be noted as that period when we began our journey into what the institutional theorists call coercive isomorphism. Simply stated, it was the beginning of a period when we let political correctness, loud boisterous voices of detached minorities, the millennial population's rejection of the ideals of their workaholic parents, the sustained bombardment of capitalism and wealth creation, and the degradation of the dignity of work force us into an homogenized economy. We are now seemingly on a long journey into an environment where politicians appease other countries by downplaying America's exceptionalism, where the idea of redistribution of wealth through taxation is gaining ground, where unwarranted advancement has denigrated elementary and high school education, and where every kid on the team gets a trophy.

While these broad generalities are anecdotal and symptomatic, and may be the fodder of debate depending on your political persuasion or personal and economic profile, one thing is clear. The United States lags the civilized world in high school graduation rates, university matriculation rates, SAT scores, math and science educational rankings, and a host of other academic measures. And in the 21st century, it has become abundantly clear that we can no longer achieve and sustain excellence by competing amongst ourselves, but rather by doing so in a global environment that transcends geopolitical, economic, and natural boundaries.

I teach graduate level business students, and I begin every semester with a simple question. How will you compete with the business school graduates from around the world given that you essentially all look alike? I remind them that they have three things in common with every student in every classroom, from London, Tokyo, Toronto, and Atlanta. First, I tell them they are all smart, otherwise they would not have successfully completed an undergraduate education and been admitted to a respected business school. Second, I tell them they all will be well educated upon graduation from their respective institutions. And finally, I remind them they all have an Intel chip in their computer. The bottom line is they will be competing for jobs and careers with people from around the world who are just as smart as they are, who have been taught by preeminent professors and are thus just as well educated as they are, and who possess the same technology as they do. So, the question becomes how will they differentiate themselves from the rest of the world in a highly competitive environment? How will they stand out in a red suit when everyone around them is wearing tan?

This book explores a path and suggests a journey that will help answer that question. In the process, it will dispel a number of myths that over the last hundred years have been ingrained in our culture and lexicon and generally have been taken for granted. Myths that have beguiled us into believing we can't challenge the status quo. Myths that seem benign, even humorous, but are insidious in undermining our ability to go beyond average, to be creative, and to be innovative. Myths that tell us to keep our heads down and work hard. Myths that remind us of our limitations, both physical and mental. Myths that suggest there are boundaries that limit what we can achieve. These myths are not secret; quite the contrary, they are well known and well accepted by many. No doubt you have heard them all your life and have, on occasion, referred to them both seriously and in jest. They are pervasive and transcend gender, age, race, and economic strata. More importantly, they impact every profession, vocation and avocation whether in the realm of business, government, education, medicine, or other professional endeavors.

Finally, this mythology that has been so ingrained in our thinking, silently and insidiously keeps us on a plateau of mediocrity. The greatest generation battled it, the Baby

Boomers learned it, and the ensuing generations of Millennials, Xers and Ys have become unknowing victims of it. It's a plateau where young people are facing the stark reality that they will not be better off economically than their parents, and where the college graduate is driven not by how much opportunity a job offers, but how balanced and fulfilling the work will be. Their future world is ensconced with middle-aged white collar employees who are settled comfortably into a cubicle life, where entrepreneurial spirit is not the domain of everyone, but is relegated to the few extraordinary thinkers who are willing to challenge the myths that serve to flatten and lengthen the road to mediocrity.

So the question looms large? How will you be different? How will you climb off the plateau? How will you bust the myths that unknowingly keep you comfortably where you are now? How will you stand out in a sea of tan suits?

First, it begins with understanding the "mythology of mediocrity" and the specific steps you can take to bust the myths and realign your thinking to ignite an entrepreneurial spirit that will guide you to embrace exceptionalism and reject mediocrity. The purpose of this book is to explore many of those age-old idioms that have become part of our vocabulary, and to demonstrate that not only are they untrue, but that you can reorient your thinking to make the "debunked" myths work to your advantage.

Let's get started.

# Curiosity

**~~Killed~~ made the Cat** Breaking the Rules and
Becoming Extraordinary

# CHAPTER 1

## Curiosity Killed the Cat (or Did It Actually Make the Cat?)

### Stir the Curious Spirit in Your Soul

Over the last several years, I have interviewed hundreds of people, some living and some now deceased, and I asked them a simple question. Have you ever owned a cat or have you ever known someone who owned a cat that died? If the answer was yes, a second question followed. Was your cat or the cat of your friends killed by curiosity? After a chuckle or two, maybe a puzzled look, and eventually the realization that my question was a serious one, the answer was, one hundred percent of the time, a resounding "No."

Curiosity never killed the cat—Curiosity was framed! But you and I have heard that expression all our lives, usually in the context of an admonition to not tread in areas where we do not belong, or as a warning that danger lurks behind a wall or around a corner. The more subtle implication is that you "shouldn't stick your nose where it doesn't belong." or you should "mind your own business." More subtle still is the notion that you simply should "stop asking so many questions." While the intended message in the old proverb may be in question, the suggested results are not; curiosity leads to dire consequences or worse.

But, back to our friend Curiosity who is now facing a rap for a crime it did not commit. It seems that Curiosity has not fared well over the years, and has been the accused culprit in many a situation. *The Phrase Dictionary* summarizes Curiosity's plight like this:

> Curiosity hasn't received a good press over the centuries. Saint Augustine wrote in Confessions, AD 397 that, in the eons before creating heaven and earth, God "fashioned hell for the inquisitive." John Clarke, in Paroemiologia, 1639, suggested that "He that pryeth into every cloud may be struck with a thunderbolt." In *Don Juan*, Lord Byron called curiosity "that low vice." That bad opinion, and the fact that cats are notoriously inquisitive, led to the source of their demise being changed from "care" to "curiosity."[1]

From Ben Johnson's *Every Man in His Humour*, to William Shakespeare's *Much Ado About Nothing*, to O. Henry's short stories, historical literature has not been kind to Curiosity. So it is no surprise that the belief of Curiosity as a suspicious or an even dangerous element has survived in our modern literature and language, and has become a common warning to young and old alike. But before considering, at least metaphorically, who *really* killed the Cat, and against overwhelming, if only circumstantial, evidence, let's consider a defense for our friend Curiosity.

Curiosity is a good thing, right? Curiosity, that emotion that makes us ask the "why" questions, that makes us want to see "one more card," that makes us try and try again, and that will not let us settle for the status quo. Curiosity that is deep within all of us, children and adults alike, and causes us to want to chase butterflies as toddlers, to explore every mud puddle we see, and later as adults to travel to distant places and to wonder about those places not yet seen. Curiosity that pushed us to find a cure for polio and is pushing us farther yet to find cures for HIV and hundreds of forms of cancer. Curiosity that even imagines remote aircraft, drones delivering packages to our front doors, automobiles that drive themselves, and commercial spaceships that explore the galaxy and return intact and undamaged. So where is the problem with curiosity? Why has it taken the rap for killing the cat? Why has historical literature painted such a dreary picture of curiosity, and why has that picture lingered in our colloquial language and proverbial sayings? More importantly, why is that driving, insatiable curiosity that we all experience as children such a rare

3

commodity in our government, our educational systems, and in the business community? What phenomenon quenches that thirst for constant learning and renders us satisfied with average grades, average performance, and average lives? Lives where we marvel at the curiosity of technology stars like Steve Jobs, Elon Musk, Michael Dell, Mark Zuckerberg and a whole host of other internet stars who seem to possess an inordinate curiosity about what can be.

Unfortunately, while all of us were born with boundless curiosity, as we grow older, it diminishes rapidly at an ever increasing rate. Professor Todd Kashdan at George Mason University believes a battle emerges between our anxious mind and our curious spirit. Our instinct to explore is tempered by our desire to conform. Professor Kashdan says, "Our curiosity and threat detection systems evolved together, and they function to ensure optimal decisions are made in an unpredictable, uncertain world. We are all motivated by the pull toward safety and seek to avoid danger, but we also possess a fundamental motivation to expand and grow as human beings."[2] The problem, in his view, is that we have devalued curiosity, putting the bulk of our energy—as individuals, communities, and nations—into anxiety avoidance. And therein lies the problem. The bulk of our energy goes toward avoiding conflict and maintaining the boundaries of our comfort zones. No wonder we marvel at those individuals who have the courage and the energy to break the boundaries and allow their curiosity to overcome their innate desire to avoid anxiety. It is not surprising that we put those exceptional individuals with entrepreneurial spirit on a pedestal and admire their ability to dream dreams and see the future before the rest of us. But are they really exceptional? Does their seemingly magical insight come from some God-given talent or is it self-taught? Could more of us be exceptional if we could find a way to break the boundaries that keep us from constantly exploring and curiously pursuing the depths of our chosen occupation or field of work?

Before we attempt to answer these questions and further explore this psychological and sometimes physical tension between curiosity and comfort, let's take a closer, less anecdotal look at how we developed our historical and modern view of curiosity.

Perhaps the most noted authority on the subject of curiosity in modern times is George Loewenstein, Professor of Psychology at Carnegie Mellon University. Professor Loewenstein, in his seminal 1994 article, *The Psychology of Curiosity*, acknowledges curiosity as a critical motivator of human behavior, both positive and negative, and notes that it has been identified as a critical or foundational element in child development, scientific discovery, art and literature, and even in commercial business.[3] He supports the anecdotal assertions of writers and philosophers centuries before noting that the definition of curiosity remained relatively stable among writers and philosophers over many centuries, with their primary focus being on the question of curiosity's moral status rather than the psychology behind it. Specifically, Loewenstein states that "curiosity as a virtue was periodically superseded by the tendency to condemn it as a vice." Loewenstein's research suggested that historically, curiosity had been defined through three separate but related views. First, it was viewed as an internally driven desire for knowledge, mostly for the sake of knowledge rather than information for some practical purpose. To quote Loewenstein, "Aristotle, for example, commented that men study science for intrinsic reasons and not for any utilitarian end."

Second, curiosity was seen as a passion conjuring up emotions around arousal and the lack of self-control. Loewenstein comments that "Cicero referred to curiosity as a passion for learning and argued that the story of Ulysses and the Sirens was really a parable about curiosity. It was the passion for learning that kept men rooted to the Siren's rocky shores."

Finally, Loewenstein notes that early scholars saw curiosity as an insatiable appetite that, if not satisfied, produced painful psychological feelings of deprivation. In essence, curiosity was an insatiable appetite for information.[4]

These prevailing attitudes all carried a rather negative connotation toward curiosity, and remained relatively consistent in postmodern times, but, in 1966, and subsequently in 1983, Hans Blumenberg, a German philosopher, published editions of *The Legitimacy of the Modern Age* in which he chronicles the "Trial of Theoretical Curiosity" from its beginning in ancient Greece through the period of Enlightenment.[5] Essentially, Blumenberg argued that curiosity began as a real virtue with the Greeks, honoring it as an intellectual way of life through the quest for knowledge about everything around them. Subsequently, in the middle ages, curiosity was deplored as a vice with the quest for knowledge quelled and often punished. Finally, curiosity began to regain its influence and credibility during the Age of Enlightenment. Professor Loewenstein explains it this way: "Curiosity's rehabilitation in the 17th century was traced to the dissemination of Galileo's discoveries. Galileo's discoveries with the telescope produced an appreciation of the knowledge enhancing the potential of scientific exploration, awareness that 'curiosity is rewarded'—the weighty significance of what had hitherto been withheld from man is confirmed, and thus the morality of self-restriction is disabused and put in the wrong."[6] In other words, in language we all understand, it is okay to seek knowledge and there should be no moral dilemma in that quest.

Perhaps you are not yet ready to acquit Curiosity for the alleged murder of the Cat, but you should now understand why Curiosity was charged in the first place, and why that mythical charge has been so difficult to prove as false. We are all born with a curious mind that is unfettered with the need for security and protection, and an intellect that boldly asks questions and enthusiastically works at solving mysteries without any clues. But, unfortunately, for most of us at some point in our lives, that insatiable curiosity that drove the entrepreneurial pioneers and thrilled us as children and adolescents gives way to acceptance. We accept that the world is the way it is, that our roles are well-defined, that we have always done it this way, and that change will be too expensive, too hard, and take too long. In other words, we settle into our comfort zones and keep our heads down and do our jobs. And along with the comfort zone comes stability, at least for a while. But then the rules somehow change; our jobs are outsourced to other countries; our managerial skill set is no longer needed in a collaborative, horizontal business structure; and we sit in our cubicles and long for the good old days. In the meantime, curiosity sits dormant waiting for that spark of imagination that will ignite it and make it shine bright again.

If we accept the premise, as most scientists do, that we are all born with some level of curiosity, what causes that curiosity to flourish in some people and to wane and almost disappear in others? What are the outside forces and influences that ignite or dampen our curiosity? Can curiosity be learned or improved? These theoretical questions—while complex and abstruse—are worth exploring even for the modestly curious mind. But there is a backdrop to the questions around curiosity that is imminently more relevant and addressable by today's managers, politicians, teachers, and aspiring business leaders. What if we could teach the tee-ball player chasing butterflies in right field to never lose that insatiable curiosity? What if we could encourage high school and college students to question the age-old idioms that their parents and grandparents grew up taking for granted? What if aspiring business leaders were rewarded for bucking the system, and embracing new, forward-looking concepts and ideas?

A noble thought you say, but aren't you a few years behind the times? The entrepreneurial spirit has never been more evident, especially in the United States. Beginning in the late 1990s, technology and innovation drove the global economy, and the commercialization of the internet has proven that companies like Google, Yahoo, Microsoft and Amazon were every bit as entrepreneurial as the pioneers of the 19th century. More importantly, you might add, these technology-driven companies are hiring and training thousands of "knowledge" workers who embody the very essence of curiosity and forward thinking. So what's to be reversed, you ask; the tee-baller has graduated to Google where he or she chases proverbial butterflies for a living.

But what if we could instill the same innovative and creative spirit seen at leading edge technology companies into every American worker in every industry, from manufacturing to financial services, retail, healthcare, or the myriad of service companies and small businesses? What if, as leaders and aspiring leaders, we could teach people to be curious and abandon the virtual but very real boundaries that constrict and inhibit their creativity and innovation? What if we could teach all our employees to think "outside-the-box"? What if we could teach ourselves to be curious?

Here's the magic...We can! If you commit yourself right now to never stop exploring, never stop asking questions, and never stop looking for a better way.

America went to the moon because Jack Kennedy was curious. The president had called a group of astronauts to the White House and he asked them if we could put a man on the moon within the decade. They said yes to Kennedy, but Alan Shepard, one of the astronauts, later said that as they left the White House, the astronauts all agreed, "this guy is nuts!"[7]

Just like Neil Armstrong and Alan Shepard, you have the same opportunity to discover new ways to do things in your company and in your profession. Even if, from time to time, some people think you are nuts!

Curiosity did not kill the Cat. Curiosity was framed. And in the next few pages I want to give you a simple action plan for igniting and releasing the curiosity that sits dormant within you. Curiosity that will help you become more effective in your job or profession, make you a more interesting person, reveal personal and professional opportunities that have been hidden, make you a better student, and help you become a more creative and potent leader. All I ask is that you keep an open mind and practice the techniques in the remainder of this chapter for at least sixty days. In the process, you will begin to teach yourself a new way of thinking and curiosity will become your friend. In fact, I hope you will conclude that Curiosity, indeed, was framed! Curiosity didn't kill the Cat; rather Curiosity *Made* the Cat.

## Imagine yourself as a curious person

Curiosity is the driver of our intellectual learning—that emotion that causes us to want to know more, to see more, and to feel more. Since most of us had a high level of curiosity as a child, only to have it dampened—if not completely extinguished—by organizational behavior, institutional norms, and standardized educational systems, we must find a way to relight the fire that drives that desire for learning. The first step is to develop an attitude of curiosity and that begins with your imagination. Start by picking a subject you are interested in and imagining what you could accomplish if you knew everything about that subject. Start with what you already know and then think about the questions you would ask to fill in the gaps in your knowledge. Most psychologists are in agreement that curiosity really occurs when we are interested in a subject about which we have a little knowledge, and there is a gap in the knowledge that we possess. As we learn more, we realize that we have been deprived of additional knowledge that may be available. Most of us have experienced this curiosity or need for information when we become anxious over health issues or have physical symptoms that might be indicative of a possible health problem. We are eager to do our own medical internet research to confirm a self-diagnosis or to relieve our fears of a serious problem. We become highly focused and our curiosity becomes almost feverish until we are satisfied we have an answer.

We are comfortable exploring and following possibilities down blind alleys in pursuit of a shred of information that will help us understand more about the issue or problem. We are comfortable because our search for information can be conducted in a private and safe environment where there is no one to criticize or call our purpose or methods into question.

Now imagine how our approach would differ if our quest for information had to be conducted in a public forum around colleagues, peers, or a boss; a forum where everything was subject to criticism and could be called into question. Notwithstanding the very private nature of our health issues, chances are we would be loath to cavalierly ask questions or follow leads down blind alleys where the results are uncertain. It is our human nature to avoid situations or actions that might subject us to criticism or call our activities into question, and it is this very tension that inhibits our curiosity in normal, everyday life. Simply put, we don't want to ask questions that make us look stupid. This tension exists in personal relationships and in work environments, but nowhere is it more evident and demonstrable than in the classroom. I teach graduate students who are smart, already well educated, with undergraduate degrees, and have a serious desire to learn. They should be, almost by definition, extremely curious. But at the beginning of a semester, most students are highly cautious and unwilling to risk asking questions in open class around a large group of other students. Only when one brave soul dares ask the question (usually one that others in the class were silently pondering as well) does it open the forum for others to chime in. The students' fear or anxiety is in direct conflict with their curiosity and their interest in gaining new information.

## Practice asking questions

The best technique for overcoming this anxiety is to take the risk and ask questions. Believe it or not, the more times you put yourself in a stressful "questioning" situation in an open forum, the more comfortable you will feel and the more developed your curiosity will become. This is why I encourage students and others to practice riding elevators "backwards" as a way of introducing themselves to strangers. Simply by walking into an elevator and introducing yourself by saying, "I am Jerry Adams with Johnson, Smith and Sims; who are you with?" opens a dialogue that will at least result in you making a new acquaintance and can often lead to new and profitable relationships. I guarantee if you try this several times in a month, your anxiety level will be dramatically reduced and your sense of curiosity will increase. Even if your first few attempts are contrived, you will find yourself genuinely interested in the people that work on other floors in your office building. One of the benefits of asking questions is that the person to whom you are talking will be impressed that you are interested in them. You only have to reflect on discussions with your spouse or someone close in your life to realize that most people appreciate someone who expresses an interest by asking questions.

I am not suggesting that you will become a "hail fellow, well met" personality overnight, but you will lessen or reduce the anxiety you feel in asking questions in an open forum, and that will, slowly but surely, hone your general attitude about curiosity. As you gain confidence by practicing the art of seeking information from others, and realizing that no one will call the Elevator Police, and that, in fact, most people will actually be pleased to engage in a conversation, especially about them, you will find yourself seamlessly transferring your new skill to all aspects of your life both personally and professionally. Remember, you were born with boundless curiosity. This exercise of learning to fearlessly ask questions is just reigniting that emotion inside you that may have been dormant too long.

## Develop a reading strategy that breeds curiosity

According to a study published in 2014 by the Pew Research Center, the average number of books read or listened to by American adults in the past year is 12 and the median number is 4.[8] In other words, half of all adults read more than 4 books and half read fewer. The researchers noted that the numbers for the prior year were consistent with their current study. The study also reported that almost one-quarter of American adults did not read a single book in 2013. This doesn't just mean that they didn't open the old hardback edition of their favorite author. They didn't open a paperback, listen to an audio book in their car, or use their Kindle or tablet to read! And if you think that is shocking, the research found that the number of non-book readers has *tripled* since 1978 (the year that Gallup reported that 42 percent of adults had read 11 books or more in the past year, and 13 percent said they'd read more than 50).

Recently, the Pew Research Center reported that just 28 percent of adults read at least 11 books.[9] Further supporting this research, a study from the U.S. Bureau of Labor Statistics found that young Americans read less than ever, with people ages 25 to 34 reading only eight minutes a day on weekends and holidays, while those 20 to 24 average around 10 minutes.[10] It may not be surprising to you that the higher the income and the greater level of education, the more books Americans read. But the reasons for so many non-readers, especially among young people, appear more obvious. The advent of the 24-hour news cycle on cable television has all but rendered the daily newspaper obsolete, especially for younger readers. Over 180 channel televisions provide them with an overwhelming amount of quick information and superficial entertainment. Perhaps more obvious is the ubiquitous "screen" that twenty-five-year-olds have grown up with, and now carry in their pockets everywhere they go. Cell phones and tablets provide the means for easy and fast communication in rapid sound bites, texts, and tweets. Who has time to sit and read a book, be it for business, education, or relaxation when you have the world in your pocket?

While it may be easy to blame technology for the decline of reading a hardback book, it is interesting that the Pew Center research also found that 87% of e-book readers and 94% of audio listeners also read at least one print book.[11] So, one might conclude that you either are a reader or you are not. Whether you are "old school" and only read hardback books, or whether you are a "techie" and only read digital print, the statistics are the same. People are reading less than they did in the last few years. Does it really matter, you might ask? You might agree with the American president character who made an appearance in the animated movie, *The Simpsons Movie*, a few years ago. When faced with a critical decision and given a stack of material to read, he said, "I was born to lead, not to read."[12] Unfortunately, the statistics do not support the view that you can be highly successful or a high achiever without reading. In fact, the evidence suggests quite the contrary. Consider the study completed by self-made millionaire Steve Siebold who interviewed 1,200 of the world's wealthiest people to determine common traits. One trait that they all had in common? They read everything from self-improvement books to autobiographies.[13]

Thomas Jefferson, in a letter to John Adams, said, "I cannot live without books."[14] Indeed, successful people thrive on reading. For them it is a portal to the unseen, a pathway to the unimagined, a hallowed ground for reflection, the breeding ground for dreams, and a steady compass for an unending journey. Great leaders have taken extraordinary steps to enter this portal unabashedly, to let it feed their curiosity and momentarily quench their insatiable need to know more. For example, Napoleon Bonaparte was a voracious reader and appointed Antoine-Alexandre Barbier as his personal librarian to create a portable library that could ensure the General had sufficient books no matter where he was in the world. He read history, fiction, poetry, religion, and geography in part to understand other cultures and to develop military campaign strategies.[15] Fast forward to Phil Knight, CEO of Nike, whose library includes volumes on Asian history, art, and poetry; and Michael Moritz, the venture capitalist who discovered Google, Yahoo, YouTube, and PayPal and took them public. Moritz says, "My wife calls me the Imelda Marcos of books (referring to the wife of former Philippines' President Ferdinand Marcos, who allegedly owned 3,000 pairs of shoes). I try to vary my reading diet and ensure that I read more fiction than nonfiction. I rarely read business books."[16]

The CEO of Berkshire Hathaway, when discussing the key to his success, pointed to a stack of books and said, "Read 500 pages like this every day. That's how knowledge works. It builds up, like compound interest. All of you can do it, but I guarantee not many of you will do it."[17]

The list of successful political and business leaders throughout history who were multi-dimensional learners with a reading strategy designed to broaden their understanding and discernment of human nature is indeed a long one. Bill Gates reads about 50 books a year; Elon Musk, the CEO of Tesla and the Founder of SpaceX, when asked how he learned to build a rocket, said, "I read books"; and Mark Zuckerberg, Founder and CEO of Facebook, announced that he was resolved to read a book every two weeks.[18]

So, the next time you mindlessly channel surf looking for *The Andy Griffith Show* or *The Big Bang Theory*, you might consider author Tom Corley's findings in his five-year study of the daily activities of 233 rich people and 128 poor people, which he wrote about in *"Rich Habits: The Daily Success Habits Of Wealthy Individuals."* He found that 67 percent of rich people watched TV one hour or less per day. So, if they are not watching TV, what are successful people doing with their "spare" time? More likely than not, they are reading. But Corley also found that successful people are not just reading anything or everything they come across. They are highly selective, and generally read more to be educated than to be entertained.[19]

In other words, they have a strategy that guides their reading. A strategy that not only rations what they are reading, but also disciplines them to find the time to read in a hectic environment where time is a precious commodity not to be wasted. The objective is simple. Think of your mind as an empty paint palette; the more you read the more the palette fills with the vivid colors that not only frame your everyday perspective, but also nourish your imagination, ignite your creativity and become the substance of your dreams. Limit your reading to only your skill set, your job, or your profession and you run the risk of developing a monochromatic palette that paints a one-dimensional caricature of who you are—or want to become. It's a caricature with only ghostly images of the curiosity and creativity that could have been.

Alternatively, develop a reading strategy that is disciplined, but without boundaries and you create a multicolored, living, self-portrait that is rich in diversity, ever changing, and always growing. Let me give you six simple techniques for developing a reading strategy that will not only breed creativity and curiosity, but will also make you a much more interesting person for others to be around.

**1. Become an avid reader of history**—Start with a book on the history of your home state or your local community. You will be amazed at the connections to be made between historical characters of your community and their descendants with whom you may want to have a relationship. It can never hurt to be able to talk with an executive in your local community about his grandfather or great grandfather. It is almost certain that the insights you gain will whet your appetite and make you curious to learn more about your community and your own heritage.

**2. Pick a subject in history and become a semi-official expert**—It may be the history of railroads, World War II, the Kings and Queens of England, Tammany Hall and the history of New York politics, or any number of other topics. The topic doesn't matter; just pick one that you find interesting. I live near Atlanta, Georgia at the foot of Kennesaw Mountain where a major battle of the American Civil War was fought. So for me, reading sufficiently to become a semi-official expert on the Civil War was a natural. Regardless of the topic, make sure you have one, and make it a journey of lifelong learning. You will be surprised at how your curiosity grows after you gain a little newfound knowledge. Perhaps just as important, you cannot underestimate the effect you can have on people around you when you become—or are perceived to be—an expert on a historical topic.

**3. Always have a biography of an important person in process**—Aspiring leaders who want to develop wider and deeper relationships appreciate that they will never become experts in human nature, but they will forever be students of human nature. Learn from leaders of the past. Get inside the mind of Winston Churchill during the terrible days of the London Blitzkrieg; understand the philosophy of Karl Marx and the demons that drove men like Joseph Stalin and Adolph Hitler; appreciate the ascent to power of Lyndon Johnson and the fall from grace of Richard Nixon; admire the courage of Mikhail Gorbachev, and the intellectual curiosity of Bill Gates. Read the stories of these leaders, whether they are good or bad, and learn from their triumphs and disasters. You may never become an expert, but your scholarship will make you a better leader in your own right, and will certainly make you a more interesting conversationalist.

**4. Find time to appreciate the arts**—Over the last twenty-five years, the business community has become a significant supporter of the arts in most major cities throughout the world. However, I am convinced as businessmen and women, our support has been proffered often to ensure our names are among the registry of honored donors, and to assuage our guilt for spending little time in enjoying the beauty or cause we so generously support. Someone has said that "art fills the potholes of the soul," and aspiring leaders could do well to take a respite from the turmoil of hectic, busy days to breathe in the beauty of the great masters who so vividly captured life on canvas. I keep a copy of *The Great Masters of European*

*Art* on my desk for that very reason. There is no need to find a museum, although a trip to the National Portrait Gallery in London will literally pump new life through your veins. I simply find a painting in the book and stare at its detail until I find myself absorbed in the challenge of reading the artist's clues to the painting's meaning and message. Try this exercise. Find an art book with the painting of *The Ambassadors*, by Hans Holbein the Younger, and linger over the objects until you have a clear sense that each one is deliberate in its placement in the picture. Then read the history of the painting. You will find, even after reading about the individual objects, that the artist has created a puzzle that will relax and perplex simultaneously. Incidentally, are you able to see the obvious, but hidden skull in the picture? You do not need to be an art connoisseur, but your library and reading strategy will be woefully lacking if you exclude the arts from either.

**5. Poetry—the aristocracy of printed words**—The poets are truly the aristocracy of all literature. They look into our souls and make us reflect on who we are and why we exist. They show us an ordinary life and reveal the extraordinary beauty of living it. The curious mind must find time to read the great poets, and to linger in prose and rhyme that soothes tired minds and replenishes bankrupt spirits. Mine the depths of T.S. Eliot's *The Wasteland*, let the shroud of twilight wrap its arms around you in Robert Frost's *Stopping by Woods on a*

*Snowy Evening*, fall in love all over again with William Shakespeare's sonnets, and reminisce over what might have been with Thomas Gray in his *Elegy Written in a Country Church Yard*. Sigmund Freud perhaps captured the need for poetry in the lives of busy capitalists, scientists, and businesspeople when he said, "Poets are masters of us ordinary men, in knowledge of the mind, because they drink at streams which we have not yet made accessible to science."[20] Make sure your reading strategy includes poetry. It will, perhaps, be out of your comfort zone, but that is the intention—to find and drink at streams that have been invisible within the boundaries of your normal routines.

**6. Read stuff outside your comfort zone**—If you are like most of us, you have your "go to" magazines or recurring subscriptions that form a portion of your monthly reading. That is great, but I want to suggest a radically different approach. You can coax your brain into more creative thinking if, rather than reading all the normal stuff, you regularly read a magazine or two that are one hundred eighty degrees from your norm. For example, you guys should occasionally read an edition of *Glamour*, *Cosmopolitan*, or *Elle*. And if you really want to get crazy, pick up a copy of *Redbook*, *Garden and Gun*, or *Southern Living*. And ladies, why not consider, once in a while, a *Gentlemen's Quarterly*, *Men's Health*, or *Maxim*. The point is to coax or even force your brain to entertain new information or at least to see the familiar from different perspectives.

While you may actually learn something new, the more important benefit of radically altering your routine is that you are teaching your brain to go beyond its normal boundaries and perhaps actually change the way it will perceive old boundaries in the future. Scientists refer to this process as neuroplasticity which means that the brain has the ability to reorganize itself by forming new neural connections especially in response to learning or experience. We will discuss this in more detail in a future chapter, but, in its simplest form, the understanding is that you really can "teach an old dog new tricks."

## Deliberately and intentionally change your routines

Most of us live and die by routine processes that we develop and perfect into demonstrable examples of efficiency. We plot the most direct and hassle-free route from our homes to our jobs aided of course by voice-activated and GPS-driven mobile devices that warn us with a calm and soothing voice when we stray from the algorithmic path the mysterious voice has selected. We arrive at our jobs and try hard to find the same parking space we occupied the day before after stopping earlier at the same Starbucks and ordering our normal grande, 170 degree, non-fat, two-pump, no-whip, upside-down caramel macchiato. Once comfortably ensconced in the cubicle—individual offices died a slow death beginning in the early 1990's—we have occupied for the last several months, we continue the daily routine that slowly, but surely, defines who we have become. It is reminiscent of the scene from the movie, *Office Space*, where Peter Gibbons, an office worker at the fictional Inatech Corporation spends the day "doing stupefyingly dull computer work in a cubicle. He goes home to an apartment sparsely furnished by IKEA and Target, and then starts for a maddening commute to work again in the morning. His coworkers in the cube farm are an annoying lot, his boss is a snide, patronizing jerk, and his days are consumed with tedium." At a particularly frustrating moment, Peter says, "Human beings were not meant to sit in little cubicles staring at computer screens all day, filling our useless forms and listening to eight different bosses drone on about mission statements."[21]

While perhaps not nearly as dramatic and demoralizing as the routine of the monotonous computer screens and "TPS" reports of *Office Space*, sometimes we all grow comfortable in familiar habits that provide necessary order to our lives, but slowly beguile us into living within boundaries where the ordinary is safe and predictable and the unexpected is scary and to be avoided. It was no doubt this very predicament that the American poet Robert Frost contemplated when he wrote these now famous and familiar lines:

*Two roads diverged in a yellow wood,*
*And sorry I could not travel both*
*And be one traveler, long I stood*
*And looked down one as far as I could*
*To where it bent in the undergrowth;*

*Then took the other, as just as fair,*
*And having perhaps the better claim,*
*Because it was grassy and wanted wear;*
*Though as for that the passing there*
*Had worn them really about the same,*

*And both that morning equally lay*
*In leaves no step had trodden black.*
*Oh, I kept the first for another day!*
*Yet knowing how way leads on to way,*
*I doubted if I should ever come back.*

*I shall be telling this with a sigh*
*Somewhere ages and ages hence:*
*Two roads diverged in a wood, and I—*
*I took the one less traveled by,*
*And that has made all the difference.*[22]

If we want to break the metaphorical cycle of "cubicle life" and regain just a modicum of that curiosity that made us chase butterflies and stomp mud puddles, then we must change and mix up our daily routines. It may be as simple as plotting a new route home from work or opting for the new tapas place for dinner, rather than your dependable burger joint. On the other hand, it may be as complicated as deciding to step into uncharted waters by changing jobs or going back to graduate school. I am reminded of an old client who was the CEO of a large advertising firm and had been married five times. He frequently reminded everyone that his creativity depended on having constant variety in his life. He was quoted as saying, "I go to bed every night with a fear that when I wake up, I will not have a new idea. So my life requires constant change in what I do and how I do it; that includes constant variety in my relationships." On a less extreme, and perhaps more reasonable scale, I was recently inspired by a colleague who after two successful careers with a large accounting firm and a Fortune 1000 company, decided to leave his position as a lecturing professor at a university to go back to school and pursue a degree in history. His reasoning: "I needed to do something different that was totally unrelated to my routine business activities."

Several things happen when you deliberately change your normal routines that have both a direct and an ancillary imprint on you. I challenge you to try the following simple three-step process for the next thirty days and decide for yourself.

- **Change the route you use to and from work on a daily basis**—If you are like me, you get in your car every morning and your brain is set on autopilot for the next hour. If you want to rekindle your curiosity, autopilot is the last thing you need. You want your brain firing and alert to every new thing your eyes see. New signs, new construction, new people, new retail shops, more inspiring views, and perhaps more challenging traffic patterns. This may require you to start just a little earlier, but the result will be worth the effort. Just for a few days, "take the scenic route."

**Extra Credit**: During this "test period", let yourself take a wrong turn on the way to work or home. Explore the new neighborhood you discover without the aid of your GPS navigation system. (You always have it if you get lost.) In addition to seeing new places, you will also be programming your brain to deal with new and stressful situations. When you are on autopilot, you are functioning with minimal conscious effort. However, when you are forcing your mind to be alert and focused on every possible twist and turn, scientists tell us that your brain can actually grow neurons as you encounter and respond to the new data. In other words, by putting yourself in new situations where you have to think, you are forcing your brain to pay attention.

- **Change the radio station that you regularly listen to while driving**—I am seriously addicted to Sirius XM radio, but until a few months ago my mornings were almost exclusively limited to a single simulcast television news show. A few months ago, however, a question occurred to me. If there are one hundred and eighty channels, what kind of people listen to the others and how are they different from me? So, I changed my routine. I started listening to a variety of stations including The Catholic Channel (for the record, I am Southern Baptist), Rural Radio, BBC World Service, and Symphony Hall just to name a few. The results are interesting. Not only did I learn new information, but I also realized that a singular focus on political news was limiting my perspective on who I am, and more importantly, on the fact that those other listeners are not so different from me. It also introduced me to new interesting subjects. A simple change in your daily listening habit may have the unexpected benefit of waking your brain to new concepts and ideas.

**Extra credit**: Occasionally, listen to a CD or audio book by a motivational author. I recommend *The Art of Exceptional Living* and *The Seasons of Life* by Jim Rohn. Jim's inspirational story and philosophy of life will spark your imagination and inspire you to change your routine.

- **Change your schedule to explore the impact of waking and retiring at different times**—Our daily work schedule usually dictates the time we get up in the morning and perhaps even the time we go to bed at night. But it does not have to mandate our schedule. This exercise is about exploring the advantages and/or disadvantages of rising and retiring at different hours than is normal for you, setting a daily schedule that is less stressful, and finding an extra hour in the day to think creatively. A study published in the Harvard Business Review, *Creativity Under the Gun*, found that creative thinking diminishes when you are under significant time pressures. The study notes that "when creativity is under the gun, it usually ends up getting killed. Although time pressure may drive people to work more and get more done, and may even make them feel more creative, it actually causes them, in general, to think less creatively."[23] Consequently, when you get up at 7 a.m. and rush to get dressed, find your briefcase, help get the kids up and dressed for school, stop at Starbucks for coffee, get to work by 9 a.m., work for ten hours, get home by 7 p.m., have dinner, get the kids ready for bed, watch TV with your spouse for an hour or so, and then fall asleep between 10 and 11 p.m., you started your day under stress and probably ended it the same way. Just for a short 30-day period, try something different. A test routine might look something like this:

- Start your day at 5:45 a.m.
- Exercise (3 days) /meditate/read (2 days) for an hour
- Plan your day for the next 15-30 minutes
- Eliminate an hour of evening television; substitute it with a book
- Lights out at 10 p.m.

Remember, I am not suggesting that this is your program forever; just for 30 days. Just long enough to jar your brain into a different routine and to find an hour or two when you and your creativity are not under the gun.

**Extra Credit**: If you are courageous enough to face the reality of how you spend or waste most of your day, try this exercise. I guarantee you will be both amazed and dismayed at the results. The real courage will come when you decide to act on the results you find. For two weeks, I want you to keep track of your time in thirty-minute increments. Use a bound notebook (analog) or any number of apps (digital) on your mobile device to write down the activity you start, when you stop and when the next activity begins. The results will give you real insight into how you spend your day but, more interestingly, into how you can harness your time to get more done and free up more stress-free time.

Imagining what curiosity looks like, developing a reading

strategy, and changing your normal routines and habits are just a few techniques that are designed to force you out of your comfort zone and help you begin a journey of reigniting the curiosity that, as a child, caused you to constantly ask those "why" questions. We were all born with a certain level of curious spirit, but somewhere along the way our brains become programmed to accept most of what we see and hear at face value, especially when we see or hear it from smart people. The fears of failure, embarrassment, retribution, looking stupid, starting over, and a host of others dampen or extinguish completely our willingness to explore the unknown or challenge the status quo. After all, we all know that Curiosity Killed the Cat!

So, if you are still reticent after considering the suggested techniques and exercises you have just read, consider for a moment, why the Cat was able to so deftly escape the clutches of Curiosity and live a full nine lives. One only has to observe or read about our feline friends to appreciate there are at least three reasons for the Cat's long-term survival. First, the Cat, as curious as he or she may be, is cautious. Second, the Cat is careful. And finally, the Cat is extraordinarily quick and nimble. The lessons for us as we begin our journey in rebuilding our curiosity should be obvious. Take bold steps, embrace the unknown, engage new concepts, abandon your metaphorical cubicle, challenge the status quo, and explore every new nook and cranny your life presents. But do it cautiously, take baby steps until you are comfortable, and be ready to react quickly as circumstances change. You will not only survive your encounters with Curiosity; Curiosity will change your life.

## The Journey to Extraordinary:
## Tips for the Traveler...

- Curiosity overwhelms mediocrity, it took us to the moon, discovered electricity, exploited the internet, conquered the genome, and it will lead you to Extraordinary.
- Chase butterflies and step in mud puddles just to remember how it feels.
- Reignite your curiosity by questioning everything you have taken for granted in the past.
- Become a serial reader. Reading is a portal to the unseen, a pathway to the unimagined, a hallowed ground for reflection, the breeding ground for dreams, and a steady compass for an unending journey.

# CHAPTER 2

# You Can't Teach an Old Dog New Tricks

## Preach Innovation

The often-quoted phrase "you can't teach an old dog new tricks" may be the oldest myth that we will explore in this book. While there is no certainty as to its origin, we do know it was mentioned as early as 1534 in Anthony Fitzherbert's *The Boke of Husbandry*, a far-ranging tome on English agriculture. Among Fitzherbert's earthy and sage advice was this verse:

"and he muste teche his dogge to barke when he wolde haue hym, to ronne when he wold haue hym, and to leue ronning, whan he wolde haue hym; or els he is not a cunninge shepeherd. The dogge must lerne it, when he is a whelpe, or els it wyl not be: for it is harde to make an olde dogge to stoupe."[24]

While the old English is tiresome, a quick freelance interpretation suggests that Fitzherbert was saying the smart shepherd knows that the young learn faster than the old and you cannot "teach an old dog to do new tricks." Regardless of its origin, the phrase has become a part of our everyday lexicon and is used frequently to excuse the obstinacy of our mothers and fathers, to take a friendly jab at a fifty-plus year old coworker who just doesn't move at our pace, or even as a crutch for our own hesitancy at taking on a new project or risky venture.

Interestingly, scientific evidence does not support the thesis that older people can't learn as much or as fast as younger people. If you are like me, you have been told, and in my case I have told others, that you cannot really change people after they reach the age of forty or so. And historically, we believed that after the age of fifty, most people were on a downhill slide. In fact, however, new scientific research contradicts the perception that older people have less ability to learn new things. The previous views were based on the belief that older people have less flexibility in their brain. This flexibility (or plasticity) is how the brain learns and retains information or knowledge. The old assumptions were that, at a certain age, we have less and less plasticity in our brains and at some point the learning and retention of knowledge or new information is essentially over, if not on a consistent decline. A new study led by Brown University researchers contradicts that view with a finding that plasticity did occur in seniors who learned a task well, but it occurred in a different part of the brain than in younger people. An article published by Brown University in 2014 summarizing the study conducted by Dr. Takeo Watanabe stated the following:

> When many older subjects learned a new visual task, the researchers found, they unexpectedly showed a significantly associated change in the white matter of the brain. White matter is the brain's "wiring," or axons, sheathed in a material called myelin that can make transmission of signals more efficient. Younger learners, meanwhile, showed plasticity in the cortex, where neuroscientists expected to see it. "We think that the degree of plasticity in the cortex gets more and more limited with older people," said Dr. Watanabe, the Fred M. Seed Professor at Brown University and a coauthor of the study published in Nature Communications. "However, they keep the ability to learn, visually at least, by changing white matter structure."[25]

Dr. Mario Garrett, Professor of Gerontology at San Diego State University, and his work on the topic of neuroplasticity, supports the Brown University findings. In *Psychology Today*, Dr. Garrett noted that "This growing evidence is popularizing the idea that the adult brain is more malleable than assumed and that it can regenerate throughout life. Decreased mental capacity is something that occurs through physical and functional changes in the brain. It can be avoided and even reversed through a variety of environmental enrichment activities, including physical and mental training exercises. The secret is to challenge the brain to do novel and stimulating tasks that do not rely on established ways of doing things."[26]

The findings of Dr. Watanabe and Dr. Garrett are just two examples of the significant research completed over the last ten years that clearly suggests that you and I may not lose our ability to learn. In fact, in many cases, it may actually be enhanced. I want you to focus again on the observation noted above by Dr. Garrett. He gives us a first glimpse into a practical way for debunking the myth that "you can't teach an old dog new tricks." He said, "The secret is to challenge the brain, to do novel and stimulating tasks that do not rely on established ways of doing things."

So let's ask the question again. Can you really teach an old dog new tricks? Can you continue learning well past age fifty or older? If so, and if Dr. Garrett's suggestion is correct, how do we unlock the secret? How do we challenge our brains to do novel and stimulating tasks that don't rely on established ways of doing things?

I believe the secret lies in a deliberate effort to **learn to be innovative**. I know you are thinking, right Larry! That's a lot easier said than done, just learn to be innovative! Or worse, you might be thinking it is impossible for me or you to *learn* to be innovative. A person is either innovative (or creative) or he/she is not. While I will agree there is no doubt some people are born with a genetic proclivity for creativity and innovation, I am also convinced that most people simply get there through a different route. Over the next few pages, I hope to persuade you that you can actually teach yourself to be more innovative and creative than you are today. It requires hard work, dedication, and discipline. You *can* learn to be an innovative thinker. The learning journey toward innovative thinking involves three action steps that are more tactical and less theoretical in nature.

## Step 1. Flatten your box

For most of your adult life, you have heard the concept of "thinking outside the box," the idea that we all live in our own little world with boundaries that govern the way we live, the way we play, and the way we approach and solve problems. But moving outside the box assumes we can simply abandon the way we think and radically change our approach to solving problems or creating new ideas. Once we have solved a problem, we simply step back in the box and resume our normal routines. This view is problematic for me. I think it is difficult, if not impossible, to simply step outside ourselves and instantaneously become a creative or innovative thinker. If it was that easy, breakthrough ideas would be ubiquitous. In fact, there are people who will go through their entire lives and never have an original thought. Perhaps the walls of their box are just too high.

Rather than thinking that you must step outside the boundaries of who you are or climb out of "your box," let me encourage you to consider another thought. Imagine that you can permanently "flatten your box." The difference may seem subtle, but the implications can be enormous. First, the boundaries go away rather than you having to step outside them. Your innovative thinking will no longer be event-based, i.e., "outside the box," it becomes pervasive and a part of who you are. Second, when your box is flattened, your perspective or distance vision improves dramatically since it is no longer obscured or limited by real or perceived obstacles. Finally, once you experience the thrill of constantly thinking about what can be, rather than what is, you will no longer need the safety of your old box.

Enough metaphorical meandering. Let's look specifically at how you can flatten your box and learn to think innovatively. Let me give you three exercises that will help you jump-start the process.

**1. Imagine there are no obstacles in your way**—In solving any major problem or resolving significant issues, my experience is that most people first think about the obstacles rather than the answer. This puts the focus on why we can't solve the problem rather than on a creative solution. For example, as a corporate board member, I have often asked a member of the management team, "What could you accomplish with this initiative if money was no object?"

Similarly, as a nonprofit board member, I have asked executive directors, "What development initiatives would you undertake if you had no financial constraints?" The concept is that once the major obstacles are removed, your mind is free to consider all the potential solutions or ideas, rather than just the ones that the constraints allow. When the obstacles are the first thing you see, your solutions become limited and your vision blurred. In my examples, the lack of funding predisposes me to the assumption that money is the only way to solve the problem when there may be alternatives that require much less money or can be solved without money.

The next time you face an issue that seems insuperable, first identify the big obstacles that seem to prevent a resolution. Then imagine those obstacles go away. What does the solution or resolution look like? What are the various alternatives that are available in the absence of the obstacle?

**2. Practice thinking three-dimensionally**—The ability to think critically and solve problems is essential to "flattening the box" and being able to think innovatively. Before defining three-dimensional thinking, it might be easier to define what it is not. Linear or binary thinking is fairly easy to understand. It means our thought process sees issues as singularly defined objects or problems that should be handled or solved one at a time in sequential order. You can't solve one issue before you solve the preceding one. In contrast, three-dimensional, multi-dimensional or lateral thinking involves solving problems by considering all the available facts or elements of a situation as a complete set and looking for connections, combinations, and permutations that allow the various elements to work in concert with each other to solve the problem. One of the simplest and most visual examples of multi-dimensional thinking is the Candle Problem, also known as Duncker's Candle Problem. The problem was created by psychologist Karl Duncker and published posthumously in 1945.[27] The problem presents the following task: how to attach and light a candle on a wall so that the candle wax doesn't drip onto the table below. One may only use the following materials together with the candle: 1) a book of matches; and 2) a box of thumbtacks.

Before turning the page, consider the image and take a few minutes to find your own solution.

Interestingly, Dr. Duncker's original participants actually had some creative ideas in solving the problem as it is presented in the image above. Some tried to use the box to tack the candle to the wall, while others tried to melt wax on the wall and stick the candle to it. The ideal solution, of course, is to take the thumbtacks out of the box and nail the box to the wall. Then the box becomes a shelf that will hold the candle as shown below.

An even more interesting demonstration of the difference between lateral and linear thinking occurred when the participants in the study were shown the same materials as in the first image except that the thumbtacks were taken out of the box and laid aside leaving the box empty. The participants almost all could then see the functional use of the box as a shelf.

Duncker noted that "The concept of functional fixedness (cognitive bias that limits a person to using an object only in the way it has been traditionally used) predicts that the participant will only see the box as a device to hold the thumbtacks and not immediately perceive it as a separate and functional component available to be used in solving the task."[28]

Now that you have seen lateral thinking in action and pictures, consider the following lateral puzzles from the book *Lateral Thinking Puzzlers* by Paul Sloane that will help you begin to feel more comfortable with multi-dimensional thinking and better understand how "flattening the box" can enlighten you to solutions that are right in front of you, but hidden to the otherwise linear mind.[29]

### Puzzle One

*A man is on his way home when he meets another man in a mask. He immediately turns around and runs the other way. What is the situation?*

### Puzzle Two

*A man pushed his car. He stopped when he reached a hotel at which point he knew he was bankrupt. Why?*

## Puzzle Three

*A man walks into a bar and asks the bartender for a glass of water. The bartender pulls out a gun and points it at the man. The man says, 'Thank you' and walks out.*

Spend a little time with these riddles. Remember, you have "flattened the box" and you are not limited to traditional definitions, traditional uses of objects, or any of the old rules that constrained your thought process. What questions do you need to ask to see the solutions? (You will find the solutions to the puzzles in the Appendix of this book.) You will be surprised at the simplicity of the answers, but don't look until you have at least tried to form a conclusion in your mind. By deliberately and routinely practicing multi-dimensional thinking, you will continually improve your critical thinking skills. It allows you to open your mind and see all the disparate elements of a problem not as individual issues, but as a set of issues that relate to each other. It also forces you to ask broad questions that will help you focus on why the problem is worth the effort to solve in the first place.

A few years ago in a meeting with the heads of acquisitions and taxation for GE Energy, a then $25 billion subsidiary of GE Corporation, we were discussing the complications of getting an audited balance sheet from an acquisition target. We were well into the weeds of how we could get the audit commissioned and completed in the time frame of the acquisition. Out of the blue, the vice president of tax said, "Let's stop for a minute and ask a metaphysical question about a balance sheet." After recognizing our puzzled looks (financial guys are rarely dealing in the world of metaphysics and even more rarely talking about it), he went on to ask, "Why a balance sheet? Let's think about why we even need a balance sheet for this deal?" After a little more discussion, we concluded that we really did not need the balance sheet. We had spent an hour or so wrestling with the question of how to make something happen that, upon reflection, was the wrong question altogether.

Some of the top-line questions you may want to ask when dealing with complicated issues include:

- Why is this significant or important?
- Do I really understand why this is a problem?
- Do we have all the information and input necessary to understand the problem?
- What will happen if we take no action?
- How do I know that the information we are seeing/sharing is accurate or complete?
- What alternatives are there to the proposed solution?
- Are we all working with the same definitions of the issue?
- How many different possibilities are there?
- What is the fundamental/driving issue creating this problem?

**3. Create collisions with diverse people**—Do you remember the old 1980's television commercial about the origin of the Reese's Peanut Butter Cup? Two people bump into each other, one holding an open jar of peanut butter and the other holding a partially-eaten chocolate bar. Each person is happy with his own unique snack, but the accidental collision of peanut butter and chocolate creates a new innovative product that seems to have the best of both worlds. Similarly, innovation can occur when two or more unique individuals with opposing personalities and ideologies collide with each other and share their different perspectives on a problem or a pending issue. In its simplest form, this means that the old adage, "two heads are better than one," is actually true. The concept of individuals sharing and collaborating with each other to create products or solve problems has proven so effective in the business community that organizations have been rapidly redesigning their office space to ensure that collaboration occurs. Private offices and conference rooms are becoming less important as large community spaces and small multifunctional spaces are designed. The break room is being replaced with in-house coffee shops and loft-like spaces with large-screen TV's, gaming tables, and comfortable sofas—all designed to promote "collisions" amongst employees on a cross-disciplinary basis.

Zappos, the large online retailer, is investing $350 million in the area around the company's new headquarters in an attempt to grow the local start-up and entrepreneurial community in a way that will organically attract talent to the area, benefiting both Zappos employees and the neighborhood. Interestingly, Zappos has created, and is experimenting with, a new metric: "collisionable hours," the number of probable interpersonal interactions that occur per hour and per acre of space. Their goal is to reach 100,000 "collisionable hours" per acre in the corporate campus and its neighborhood, representing about 2.3 collisions per square foot, per year.[30] Why is this so important? Because when people are interacting or colliding with each other with different backgrounds, socio-economic status, ethnicity, work experiences, and ideologies, good things happen. Innovation occurs. Creativity blossoms. Ideas are nourished. It is relevant, not only at a corporate level, but at a personal one as well. That's where you come in. If you want to become more innovative, you have to seek out opportunities where you can "collide" with a different and diverse group of people. Fortunately, this is not hard, because they are all around you—where you work, where you shop, where you worship, where you play, and where you go to school. But collisions don't just happen. Just as Zappos has to force an environment that creates collisions, you have to take deliberate steps to ensure that personal collisions become a part of your everyday routine.

Let me give you three ideas:

- **Set a goal of having lunch with at least one "new person" each week**—It never ceases to amaze me how much time busy people waste on lunch. Now don't get me wrong, I appreciate a casual lunch with friends or business associates as much as anyone. I even treasure the occasional lunch by myself when I can read or just think without the obligation of communicating with someone else. But if you are interested in accelerating your innovative thinking, let me challenge you to take advantage of the purpose-driven lunch. The very title should suggest that this hour in the day does not "just happen" or occur haphazardly or without some amount of planning. Planning is necessary because our human nature defaults to the "known," the people we know, the topics we are accustomed to discussing with them, and the places we are comfortable going to together. Like the old television show, *Cheers*, we want to go "where everyone knows our name." But innovation occurs at the intersection of the known and unknown, and interacting with people who are different than us can often be the catalyst to spark a new idea or a creative thought.

We are different because of our socioeconomic background, our education, our religious upbringing, and the anecdotal and informal learning from our grandmothers on our father's side. Your perspective on things may be completely different than mine because I played Little League baseball as a kid and you took piano lessons; I read a Helen Fuller Orton mystery book and you read Silas Marner. When we intentionally collide with new people and share ideas, we can dip into this diversity and broaden our perspective in a way that self-debate and introspection never can. But if you think I am suggesting you begin stopping people on the street or doing internet searches for strange people, let me put your mind at ease. No such search is necessary. There is a world of diversity at your fingertips. The people in other departments where you work, the classmates in school that you rarely speak to, the businessman at church who you would like to know better but have never taken the time to meet, or the other countless number of people that you see daily in some capacity or another. If you think about it, when it comes to an inventory of diverse people to meet, you are "sitting on a ham sandwich and starving to death." So just get started. The first one will be the hardest, but it will whet your appetite to take another bite.

- **Avoid a "silo" mentality and embrace collaboration—** The idea of collaboration and its effect on innovation is not new. Business leaders, educators, and politicians all recognize the importance of collaborating to get things done faster and more efficiently, but they still struggle at making it happen. You only have to consider the current political environment in the U. S. Congress to understand how difficult it is to collaborate on solving problems. The ratings organization, Nielsen Media Research, did a study of Consumer Package Goods (CPG) professionals and noted in a preface to the study that "two out of every three front-line CPG professionals rank collaboration as one of the top five most critical factors to innovation success, yet the majority of companies still struggle to collaborate effectively."[31] If the most powerful people in government and the most respected companies in the world find it difficult to collaborate, no wonder we, as individuals, tend to stay in our silos rather than collaborate with others. Some of the reasons for our hesitancy may be that we have been taught, from childhood, to learn independence, dress yourself, tie your own shoes, be a self-starter, and "do it yourself." We all know "the early bird gets the worm" and the old saying was reinforced as we competed in a "dog eat dog" world where it's "every man for himself." But what if we could get more worms, or more of what we want, if we could find a way to collaborate with those around us rather than going it alone. The best example of this is a scientific one, but comes from a popular movie that you may remember.

John Nash, a mathematician at Princeton University, is played by Russell Crowe in the movie *A Beautiful Mind*. In the film, Nash tries to explain game theory and his belief that Adam Smith was wrong when he proposed in his book, *A Wealth of Nations*, that the best result comes when a person works to his own self-interest.[32] In other words, the greatest result occurs because a person is in it for himself. Nash believed that Adam Smith's theories needed revision in that the best answer or greatest result comes when a person works in his own best interest *and* in the interest of the greater group. His theory was that the pie gets larger when a group works together, rather than alone. In a scene from the movie, Dr. Nash is at a bar with three friends, and they are all enraptured by a beautiful blonde woman who walks in with three brunette friends. While his friends banter about which of them would successfully woo the blonde, Dr. Nash concludes they should do the opposite: ignore her. "If we all go for the blonde," he says, "we block each other and not a single one of us is going to get her. So then we go for her friends, but they will all give us the cold shoulder because nobody likes to be second choice. Well, what if no one goes for the blonde? We don't get in each other's way and we don't insult the other girls. That's the only way we win. Adam Smith needs revision."[33] As it turned out, Nash won a Nobel Prize for his equilibrium theory (the Nash equilibrium) which gained wide acceptance in its application to economics and the social sciences. For you and me, there is a lesson on collaboration. If Nash was right, and we can collaborate on an idea or a problem with others, we will achieve greater success than if we work on the same issue or problem as individuals. I encourage you to embrace collaboration as a tool in dealing with personal or business issues. Collaboration will facilitate your innovation both in the breadth, depth and speed of your solutions.

- **Intentionally seek the views of people who disagree with you**—Friedrich Wilhelm Nietzsche, a German philosopher of the nineteenth century once said, "He who cannot put his thoughts on ice should not enter into the heat of dispute."[34] One of the most important tools in building an innovative thought process is the courage to genuinely listen to others who disagree with your proposals or thesis. If your ideas generate no opposition or opposing views, you may have no one listening or you may be in danger of falling into Group-think, a term coined by psychologist Irving Janis in 1972 to describe a process by which a group can make irrational decisions because each person in the group tends to conform their opinions to what they want the group to hear.[35] Let me encourage you to proactively seek the opinions of those who disagree with you. The vigorous debate will accomplish at least three things. First, it provides a vehicle for pressuring yourself to test your assumptions and conclusions with others. Second, it can be a portal for opening your mind to refinements of your original thoughts. And finally, healthy debate can serve to reinforce your current position on an idea or thought and fuel the energy you might need to move it to the next level or to final conclusion. Disagreement is not conflict. Embrace it, encourage it and act upon it. Remember, innovation and creativity occurs at the intersection or collision of diverse ideas.

## Step 2. Practice failure

Most of us live in fear of failure and it's not hard to understand why. We grew up in environments where the emphasis was on winning and being first. Whether it was report cards from elementary school, cheerleading competition, or sports teams tryouts, making the grade and making the team was big-time important. The emphasis on winning did not change as you grew older. The stigma of not being accepted by the fraternity or sorority, the self-kept secret of the mediocre SAT score, and the rejection by a college or university all served to reinforce in your mind one simple, undisputable fact—failure sucks! Unfortunately, failures like these—ingrained in us from past events—have a long shelf life.

I can still recall the very day, over fifty years ago, when Coach Mike Garvin called me aside at a baseball tryout and let me know that I would not make the team. I had been "cut." I was a failure, and I never made another attempt to play organized baseball.

If you think the shelf life of failure is limited to those impressionable days of youth, fast forward some thirty-five years later when the CEO of one of my largest clients at Price Waterhouse (now the international accounting firm PwC) called me into his office to say that our fifteen-year relationship was over and that my firm was being replaced with another large accounting firm. I had been fired! There is rarely a month that goes by that I do not still remember that spectacular, sunshine-filled spring day in North Georgia when I was informed that I was a failure in client service.

So let's all agree, there is nothing good about failure, right? Failure sucks! After all, we all know the famous quote from coach Vince Lombardi of the Green Bay Packers: "Winning isn't everything, it's the only thing." And so not winning results in losing. And losing makes you a Failure with a capital F.

And then there is the real risk of failure that we face every day. The risk of embarrassment when we say something stupid in a meeting, the risk of not getting the promotion, the risk of failing an exam, the risk of a proposal not being accepted, and a multitude of other situations where failure lurks. Why then, you might ask, should I entertain the idea of "practicing failure?" And, by the way, what do you mean by "practicing" failure?

Practice usually implies that if I do it over and over, I might get better at it, or at least gain something from it. Dr. Sim Sitkin, Professor of Management at Duke University's Fuqua School of Business introduced the phrase "intelligent failure" in his 1992 publication *Learning Through Failure—The Strategy of Small Losses*. Dr. Sitkin proposed the idea that rather than learning how to succeed by avoiding failure, we should consider a new model that focuses on learning through experimentation.[36] In other words, we should accept the fact that the process of learning must include little failures along the way. This thought was reinforced by Dr. Jack V. Matson, Professor Emeritus at Penn State University, in his concept of "intelligent fast failure," which he considered a teaching tool for creativity and innovation. Dr. Matson argued that "it is important to understand that the breakthrough of creativity and innovation is based on knowledge acquisition and fast failures… which are the essential elements of the learning process."[37]

The practical application of these theoretical concepts is that failure should be embraced as a natural part of your quest to become an innovative thinker. Rather than focusing on failure, the emphasis should be on the trial and error aspects of challenging, testing, and refining ideas and solutions. In short, the failure or success model is replaced with the experimentation model.

In our quest for creativity and innovation, failure becomes our friend. In your personal quest to become an innovative thinker and "learn new tricks," let me offer three ideas you can try.

**1. Commit yourself to using failure as a learning tool**— Remember that Walt Disney was fired from a newspaper because he was told he lacked creativity. Shortly thereafter, he formed a company, *Laugh-O-Gram*, which he was later forced to close.[38] Milton Hershey started three candy companies and watched them all fail before founding The Hershey Company, and launching the Hershey Bar. Stephen King, the Master of Horror and bestselling author, had thirty rejections of his first book, *Carrie*. He had decided to give up, and literally threw the manuscript into the garbage. His wife retrieved it from the wastebasket and convinced him to resubmit the manuscript one more time.[39] The rest is history and King now has published over fifty bestselling novels. There are hundreds of other examples including Jim Carrey, Oprah Winfrey, Bill Gates, Thomas Edison, and Henry Ford. All demonstrated proof that failure is a powerful teacher. The takeaway from these examples: failure may look like the end of your story, when, in fact, it is just the beginning.

**2. Review your most recent failures and write down what you learned**—I am a firm believer that experience alone is not worth very much. The only thing it guarantees is that you will have more of it the longer you live. My golf game is evidence enough that playing a lot of golf does not, necessarily, make you a better golfer. However, when you gain experience and have a plan to proactively learn from it, and then put the learning into practice, experience takes on a whole new meaning. Henry Petroski, a Professor at Duke University and engineer who specializes in failure analysis, says, "With each tottering attempt to walk, our bodies learn from the falls what not to do the next time. In time, we walk without thinking and think without falling, but it is not so much that we have learned to walk as we have learned not to fall."[40] When you try something new and fail, or when you fail over and over, take time to explore what you did right and wrong, and why it didn't work that time. Take notes and revisit them to refocus your efforts.

3. **Celebrate your failures**—Sara Blakely, Founder and CEO of Spanx, says when she was growing up and she told her dad about a personal failure, he would high five her and say, "way to go!"[41] The attitude of celebrating mistakes, missteps, or embarrassments is simply a process of reframing failure into a temporary stepping-stone to the next success. When asked if he felt like a failure after having gone through over 1,000 failed attempts to create what became known as the light bulb, Thomas Edison simply stated "Why should I feel like a failure? And why would I ever give up? I now know definitely over 1,000 ways an electric light bulb will *not* work. Success is almost in my grasp!"[42] Celebrate failure for the nuggets of information you learn from it, and try, try again.

## Step 3. Become an expert in some subject

On our journey to innovative thinking, we have explored the concept of "flattening your box" and reframing our failures only as stepping-stones to the next success. Now let's go slightly deeper.

I want you to pick a subject and, over time, become at least a semi-official expert in that topic. Start by learning a little and then begin focusing more and more in greater detail. The topic doesn't matter. Just make sure you have one in which you are genuinely interested and make it a journey of lifelong learning and sharing with others. The magic is not just in the information you will learn. The process will facilitate the neuroplasticity of your brain as your expanded education creates a "knowledge gap" between what you have learned and the vast amount of information you realize is still to be learned. This knowledge gap can be the energy that fuels and challenges your brain to learn new concepts, gain new information, and retain its plasticity and ability to continue learning well into "old" age. In other words, the old dog will continue to learn new "tricks."

## The Journey to Extraordinary:
## Tips for the Traveler...

You are never too old, too talented or too experienced to learn new "tricks." The key is to embrace innovation, seek interpersonal collisions with people different from you, practice and celebrate failure and become an expert in the subject of your choosing. Rather than thinking "outside the box", flatten your box to provide greater visibility in problem solving. As an interesting exercise, take a group to one of the many escape rooms in your town, where you and your friends have to work collaboratively to solve a multitude of problems and puzzles before you can escape the room. Afterwards, reflect on the three-dimensional thought required to be successful.

# CHAPTER 3

## Don't Count Your Chickens Before They Hatch

### Reignite your Dreams

"Don't count your chickens before they hatch" is one of the oldest myths we will consider in our quest to rewrite the rules that erect boundary stakes around our thinking, and inhibit our ability to break free and become extraordinary. While the original author of the saying is uncertain, we do know that it was recorded in print in 1570 by Thomas Howell in *New Sonnets and Pretty Pamphlets*.[43] Samuel Butler also recorded the thought in 1664 in his poem *Hudibras*: "To swallow gudgeons ere they're catch'd, and count their chickens ere they're hatched."[44] While the origin might be in question, there is little doubt as to its meaning in both the old English and our current language. A wise person never counts on a desired—or otherwise perceived as likely—outcome until the event is an absolute certainty. Don't let your expectations get ahead of reality! As Clint Eastwood reminded us in the old movie, *Dirty Harry*, "A man has to know his limitations!"[45]

Hopefully, after reading chapters one and two, you are already questioning the thesis of both Thomas Howell and Dirty Harry. Why should I let anyone define my limitations? Why can't I approach life with a positive belief that I can exceed expectations? That I can achieve the extraordinary, and that I can see the result before it happens. Professional golfers talk about their approach to every golf shot they make. They first visualize the shot they want to make and see the trajectory of the ball flight in their mind. Then they "feel" the shot where they imagine what the emotional experience associated with the successful shot will be. Finally, they trust the shot. They trust the thousands of practice swings they have made that will be just like this one. They are absolutely counting their chickens before they hatch. But it is not some offhand roll of the dice or random luck they are counting on. It's developing a positive attitude that does not put limitations on one's abilities, but rather creates a vision of what can be that is supported by the diligence and hard work that preceded the swing.

In your business and personal life, you have been often told you should never count your chickens before they hatch. Your budgets should be conservative, your plans reasonable, and your expectations for the future tempered. Unfortunately, as wise as that approach might sound, it is a tried and true recipe for becoming average; an absolute guarantee that the results will be ordinary or, at best, "meet expectations." So, in our quest to become extraordinary, let's break the rules. Let's abandon the admonition that we should not count our chickens before they hatch. Let's retrain ourselves to dream and make those dreams our weapon of choice to defeat Average or Ordinary. Retraining is necessary because Average and Ordinary are all around us. Over time, the more educated we become and the smarter we get, the more we come to believe in our limitations; and the more we come to accept that there are simply some goals too hard to accomplish, some stars too far to reach, and some dreams too wild to believe.

Steven Pressfield, an author of several novels including *Gates of Fire* about the Battle of Thermopylae (aka the movie *300*), wrote a nonfiction work titled, *Do the Work*. In it, he implores his reader to "Stay Stupid. The three dumbest guys I can think of: Charles Lindbergh, Steve Jobs, and Winston Churchill. Why? Because any smart person who understood how impossibly arduous were the tasks they had set themselves would have pulled the plug before he even began. Ignorance and arrogance are the artist and entrepreneur's indispensable allies. She must be clueless enough to have no idea how difficult her enterprise is going to be—and cocky enough to believe she can pull it off anyway. How do we achieve this state of mind? By staying stupid. By not allowing ourselves to think. A child has no trouble believing the unbelievable, nor does the genius or the madman. It's only you and I, with our big brains and our tiny hearts, who doubt and overthink and hesitate. Don't think. Act."[46]

So in our quest to be Extraordinary, let me encourage you to learn to dream. If you are a dreamer that has been discouraged by cubicle life or the obstacles in your environment, then commit to "redreaming your dream," whatever it might be. Regardless of the dreams, there are three imperatives that will help make them a reality. Dreams demand a willing traveler, require a plan, and should be big. Let's consider each of them.

## 1. The Willing Traveler—
## Dreams are the GPS of your Soul

Most of us are, at best, part-time dreamers if at all. We opt early for the practical, for the paycheck. Our parents implore us to find a major in college that will produce a job at the end of four years. I was not different. When I graduated from high school, I wanted to become a teacher. But everyone knew you could barely make a living teaching school. So, I put the dream on hold for thirty-seven years while I pursued a career in business and accounting. I put it on hold, but it did not die. Upon retirement from PwC, I almost immediately began teaching graduate-level courses at Kennesaw State University. While I enjoyed my successful career in public accounting at one of the largest accounting firms in the world, today there is nothing more joyful than walking into a classroom full of MBA students. I often tell people that every single time I walk into the classroom I feel like a five-year-old on Christmas morning.

It was probably this delayed dream that changed the way I handled both of my children when it came time for them to make big decisions about school and work. My son, Jay, informed my wife and me a few weeks before high school graduation that he and four friends had decided not to go to college, but rather to take their band, Rare Breed, on the road. After much deliberation, a few weeks later, they loaded all their gear into a sixteen-foot rented truck and headed off for their first gig in Vidalia, Georgia. I was able to negotiate an agreement with the group that if the band did not have a record contract in one year, they would all go to college. Interestingly enough, at the end of one year, almost to the day, Jay began school at Berklee College of Music. He pursued his dream of writing songs and making music, and still does today, although as an avocation rather than a vocation.

Similarly, a few years later my daughter, Keri Lynn, was grappling with whether she wanted to remain with a large national newspaper as their South Florida Advertising Sales Manager or give up a handsome salary and enter film school to pursue a career in making movies. One new year's day morning after asking, "Dad, what should I do?" I penned the following prose and sent it to her as my answer:

## A Victorian Sunday Afternoon

*The New Year brings reflection on the past, and a nostalgic sense that the past was better than the present. Ah! Those by-gone days of old, when life was simple and idyllic like a picture of a Victorian Sunday afternoon with a picnic by the lake, with small boats sailing and smaller children playing. But we only realize much too late that life is not a Victorian Sunday afternoon and the glorious past was not nearly as glorious as the mirrored images our minds reflect. So we come to a new year with a clean slate that can be painted upon as we please. But, the slate only remains clean for an instant as we color it with what we do, and alas what we choose not to do. What choices to make? It's a game we play. What will we do this year that is different from the last? What new skill will we learn? What resolutions will we aspire to keep in the face of obstacles of time and space that resolve, to undo the resolved matter before it is nurtured beyond incubation? So we find ourselves at a juncture of past and present, of yesterday and tomorrow, of what was, and is, and what will be. And for this fleeting moment you can look again at the clean slate and find a palette of color that only you can see. But do it quickly before the gauzy images of nostalgic ghosts remind you of your responsibilities and your limitations and your expectations of life on a Victorian Sunday afternoon. Do it quickly because in a moment the slate will reflect a new picture with new lines and new colors. Do it quickly before the obstacles become permanent obstructions, and the fragrance of a new morning becomes the stale remnant of a wasted afternoon. Do it quickly before the ever-changing landscape you imagine becomes the familiar paint by numbers portrait you have become.*

Keri Lynn almost immediately quit her job and started film school. After graduation, she made numerous movies including her feature film, *Lost Angel*, that won several awards at film festivals including Best Indie Feature and her short film, *Unconditional*, that screened at the Cannes Film Festival.

Dreams are the GPS of your soul. They keep your head in touch with your heart and they ultimately become the source of your fulfillment. Sometimes they may be a distant star, but always a beacon that calls to you and beckons you home where your passions and skills can collide to make your dreams come true. In your quest to become Extraordinary, let yourself become a willing traveler. Spend time identifying the dreams that matter most to you and the skills that will be required to make them happen. Dreams don't come true through wishing and hoping. They require hard work, dedication, sacrifice, and a commitment to follow them for the long haul, regardless of their meandering path. Identifying your dreams and becoming a willing traveler—setting your internal "GPS" coordinates to their destination—can be the catalyst for crushing Average, shattering Ordinary, and becoming Extraordinary in whatever you do.

Identifying and documenting your dreams and imagining their destination will help you accomplish the following practical steps in your journey to success.

- **Connect you with your passions**—Magic happens when you are able to find that conjunction of your passions, skills, and God-given talents; that illusive spot where your natural talents and your learned skills combine with your unbridled enthusiasm to drive you toward an objective.

Identifying and embracing your dreams will give definitive mission to your passion and allow you to harness skills that education and experience have taught you; they will help you identify and resurrect talents that may have lain dormant awaiting this point. The magic occurs when you are able to connect your head with your heart and begin to formulate a plan with a timeline and action steps.

- **Motivate yourself to exceed your limitations**—The process of identifying and cataloging your skills and talents will help you come face-to-face with both your internal and external limitations. What are the barriers and obstacles that will prevent or inhibit you from achieving your dreams? Are they emotional or physical? How much of the perceived limitation is self-imposed?

There is no doubt that each of us has emotional and physical limitations. I know, for example, that no matter how much I dream about being a scratch golfer, I will never physically have the strength, flexibility, or hip rotation to hit the ball like Rory McIlroy. I know for a fact, however, that I can overcome some of the emotional obstacles that limit my golf score. If you are a golfer, you too have called upon this inexplicable "Jedi mind trick." Why is it that after I hit a miserable shot and yell profanities at myself, I can instinctively drop another ball and hit the shot perfectly? Either I or one of my partners will, no doubt, chime in and say, "Yep, Bubba can always do it." Why is it that the mythical "Bubba" who lives inside every golfer can emerge and hit the perfect shot? My anecdotal explanation is that Bubba overcomes the limitations of his alter ego, namely the real me. As he drops the ball on the ground, all the tension leaves his body, the fear of hitting a bad shot disappears, his hands are no longer gripping the club in a death choke, the stakes have been lowered, and his mind can now operationalize the feedback from the previous swing. If this is true in a golf game, might the concept also apply to more meaningful activities in the pursuit of our dreams?

Interestingly, psychologists have discovered that the answer is a resounding yes. In an article published in *Scientific American* in 2013, "Your Thoughts Can Release Abilities beyond Normal Limits," Ozgun Atasoy asserts "Our cognitive and physical abilities are in general limited, but our conceptions of the nature and extent of those limits may need revising. In many cases, thinking that we are limited is itself a limiting factor. There is accumulating evidence that suggests that our thoughts are often capable of extending our cognitive and physical limits."[47] Atasoy goes on to review numerous scientific studies including one where certain groups were asked to answer a question that would flash on a screen. "People in one group were told that, before each question, the answer would be briefly flashed on their screens—too quickly to consciously perceive, but slow enough for their unconscious to take it in. The other group was told that the flashes simply signaled the next question. In fact, for both groups, a random string of letters, not the answers, was flashed. But, remarkably, the people who thought the answers were flashed did better on the test. Expecting to know the answers made people more likely to get the answers right."[48] This and other similar studies suggest that, in fact, our mindset can help us overcome our perceived limitations. As you assess the skills you need to achieve your dreams, start with the belief that there are no limiting factors to your success. When you discover limitations you cannot overcome, you will be better prepared to find alternative solutions or call on other resources for help.

- **Accelerate your sense of urgency**—When you identify and document your big dreams, you should find a way to keep a reminder of them visibly in front of you. Whether a notepad on your desk, a screensaver on your computer, or a sign hung on your wall, we all need a constant reminder of what is important to us. The reason is simple. It is our human nature to get caught up in short-term projects or issues that in the heat of the moment appear more urgent than they probably are. Your big dreams are more likely to be long-term and, conversely, they are easy to put on the back burner in favor of the shorter-term objectives. By identifying your dreams and making them visible, you can accelerate your sense of urgency around them.

## 2. Dreams require a plan

Dreams that stay in the back of your mind, even if you have identified and documented them, are just rainbows and illusions unless you have a plan to bring them to life. When you reach that enviable position where your heart has connected with your head and you are ready to pursue what really matters to you, it is not enough to just talk about it. In fact, there are some psychologists who suggest that talking about your dream is the worst thing you can do—that keeping it secret will motivate you to work toward it. Regardless of your approach, you must have a well-thought-out plan that will provide direction for your plotted GPS coordinates, create a means for measuring your progress and establish the specific steps required to make your dream a reality. Let me suggest a personal framework I have found helpful in planning big missions, focusing my attention on critical action steps and in monitoring my progress.

In the chart shown, note the four separate phases of your big dream planning process:

**Phase I**—Articulate your dream in a mission statement that is concise, clear, and descriptive.

**Phase II**—Establish at least three—but no more than four—objectives that will need to be accomplished before reaching your dream. These will be precursors to your plan and are designed to provide focused direction to your efforts. *This phase is dream or mission critical.*

**Phase III**—Identify at least three specific goals that you must accomplish for each of the established objectives. Your objectives may be multifaceted and have a fair amount of flexibility in how they are accomplished. Hence, your goals

# ARTICULATE YOUR OWN BIG DREAM HERE

**Sample Dream:** Write and publish a murder mystery set in the north Georgia mountains with a story line about the region's Native American heritage and the unique characters that dominate mountain life.

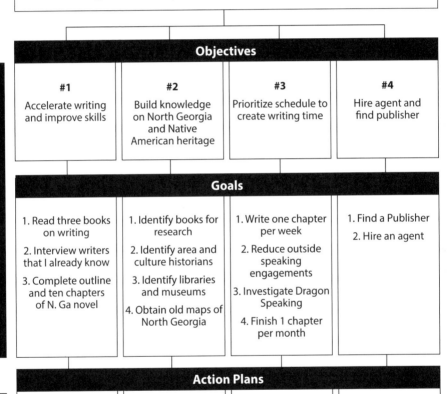

**DREAM CRITICAL**

**MEASURABLE**

## Objectives

**#1**
Accelerate writing and improve skills

**#2**
Build knowledge on North Georgia and Native American heritage

**#3**
Prioritize schedule to create writing time

**#4**
Hire agent and find publisher

## Goals

1. Read three books on writing

2. Interview writers that I already know

3. Complete outline and ten chapters of N. Ga novel

1. Identify books for research

2. Identify area and culture historians

3. Identify libraries and museums

4. Obtain old maps of North Georgia

1. Write one chapter per week

2. Reduce outside speaking engagements

3. Investigate Dragon Speaking

4. Finish 1 chapter per month

1. Find a Publisher

2. Hire an agent

## Action Plans

1. Explore alternative writing techniques

2. Complete outline by June 1

3. Complete book draft by December 1

1. Complete major research by March 1

2. Hire a graduate assistant to assist with research

3. Meet curator at Atlanta History Museum by Jan 1

4. Visit Rabun County Library by Jan 15

1. Commit to 1500 words per day

2. Establish daily writing routine

3. Reduce outside meetings to five per week

4. Resign two nonprofit boards for year

1. Identify potential agents

2. Identify all possible publishers

3. Draft proposal for submission to publishers by June 1

need to be very specific and targeted towards enhancing your knowledge or acquiring skills you will need to be successful.

**Phase IV**—Establish specific action plans that you must complete in order to reach your established goals. It is absolutely essential that these plans be targeted and **measurable**. Measurable goals will keep you focused and help you stay on track. If possible, the goals should have benchmarks or time frames attached.

Remember, the sample framework is fictional and just an example. Experiment with your own chart. It is not a substitute for the passion, skills, and talents you will need to turn your dreams into reality, but it is a great road map for planning, monitoring, and measuring your journey.

### 3. Finally, always dream big

Hopefully, you are ready to abandon the old saying, "Don't count your chickens before they hatch," and begin a journey of creating dreams and making them a reality. I want to leave you with some words of encouragement as you begin. Always dream big! Even if you think the dream is impossible. Walt Disney once said, "All our dreams can come true if we have the courage to pursue them."[49] Interestingly, when Steve Jobs was asked by a Disney executive about plans for revitalizing the Disney Stores, Jobs said, "dream bigger."[50] Your dreams are inspirational not only for you, but for all those around you; no one gets inspired by modest dreams. The bigger your ambition, the bolder your dream, the higher your goal, the more you will achieve.

In a study entitled, *Ain't No Mountain High Enough? Setting High Weight Loss Goals Predict Effort and Short-Term Weight Loss*, scientists wanted to test the "modest goal" theory. They explored whether the amount of weight loss individuals strive for is associated with more positive psychological and behavioral outcomes. Over four hundred overweight and obese participants trying to lose weight were surveyed about their weight loss goals and progress over a two-month interval.

According to the researchers, "Many participants set goals that could be considered unrealistically high. However, higher weight loss goals predicted more effort in the weight loss attempt, as well as more self-reported short-term weight loss."[51] In plain English, the study revealed that those subjects that set the biggest weight loss goals achieved the best results and worked harder to achieve them.

As a businessperson, I have always encouraged "stretch goals" which are goals that are bigger than budgets and perhaps just a little beyond the reach of ordinary efforts. My experience is that we usually achieve what we set out to achieve. So why not aim a little higher? The worst that can happen is we achieve the ordinary. But we might just go well beyond and achieve the extraordinary. Remember, your dreams are your weapons against average.

History is littered with ordinary people who had big

dreams. Whether it's the Wright brothers who dreamed of a flying machine, Sam Walton who wanted to give "poor people the chance to own the same stuff that rich people have," Bill Gates who dreamed of putting a computer in the hands of everyone, or Thomas Edison who tried 1,000 times before he finally succeeded in inventing the light bulb, they all had one thing in common. They dreamed it, they believed it, and their hard work made it happen. Napoleon Hill, in his book, *Think and Grow Rich*, said, "Thoughts are Things."[52] If you are a dreamer, think big thoughts. Write your dreams down and make a plan to help accomplish them. Don't let people discourage you. If they think you are crazy, if they encourage you to "know your limitations" or tell you to "act your age," go read the commencement speech that Steve Jobs gave at a Stanford graduation in 2005. Here is what he said, "Stewart Brand and his team put out several issues of The *Whole Earth Catalog*, and then, when it had run its course, they put out a final issue. It was the mid-1970s, and I was your age. On the back cover of their final issue was a photograph of an early morning country road, the kind you might find yourself hitchhiking on if you were so adventurous. Beneath it were the words: 'Stay Hungry. Stay Foolish.' It was their farewell message as they signed off. Stay Hungry. Stay Foolish. And I have always wished that for myself. And now, as you graduate to begin anew, I wish that for you."[53]

Stay Hungry. Stay Foolish. And keep dreaming!

## The Journey to Extraordinary:
## Tips for the Traveler...

Dreams are the GPS of your soul, but they require a willing traveler. Take time to give substance to your dreams. In the midst of your busy, hectic schedule, take time to prepare a three-point plan of actions you need to take to make your dreams come true; if you can dream it, you can do it.

# CHAPTER 4

## A Little Learning is a Dangerous Thing

### Seek Diversity

Another myth that has been around for a few centuries and has become embedded in our everyday language is the old saying, "A little knowledge is a dangerous thing." At the risk of giving you the impression that we are delving too deeply into English literature, let me provide a bit of background on the history of this old saying. The English poet philosopher Alexander Pope wrote the following verses as part of a much larger poem published in 1704 called an "Essay on Criticism."

### A Little Learning

*A little learning is a dangerous thing;*
*Drink deep, or taste not the Pierian spring:*
*There shallow draughts intoxicate the brain,*

*And drinking largely sobers us again.*
*Fired at first sight with what the Muse imparts,*
*In fearless youth we tempt the heights of Arts;*
*While from the bounded level of our mind*
*Short views we take, nor see the lengths behind,*
*But, more advanced, behold with strange surprise*
*New distant scenes of endless science rise!*
*So pleased at first the towering Alps we try,*
*Mount o'er the vales, and seem to tread the sky;*
*The eternal snows appear already past,*
*And the first clouds and mountains seem the last;*
*But those attained, we tremble to survey*
*The growing labours of the lengthened way;*
*The increasing prospect tires our wandering eyes,*
*Hills peep o'er hills, and Alps on Alps arise!*[54]

Pope's first and most famous line of the poem, "A little learning is a dangerous thing" has often been misquoted over the years and has almost always been interpreted as a discouragement for someone to learn or gain superficial knowledge about a given subject. The opinion is, of course, that a little knowledge might be just enough to get you in trouble and certainly you should be wary of a person with "just enough" knowledge. A closer look at Pope's "Essay," however, suggests that he may have intended a deeper or at least an additional meaning. The poetry is rich with the idea that a little learning will whet your appetite for more and more knowledge. The poet speaks of "New distant scenes of endless science" and says in the final verse, "The increasing prospect tires our wandering eyes, Hills peep o'er hills, and Alps on Alps arise!" In other words, the horizon is endless with mountain peaks only leading to higher mountain peaks; the more we learn, the more we realize how much there is yet to learn.

In my book, *Riding Elevators Backwards*, I said that Alexander Pope, with his "A little learning is a dangerous thing," was dead wrong and I postulated that a little learning can be a wonderful thing. In fact, I must beg the poet's forgiveness. Pope was not so much saying that a little learning is a terrible thing, but rather that a little learning is simply inadequate when there is so much more to learn. Pope was actually highly critical of those poetry critics of his day who argued that so many of the poets were not maintaining the proper bounds of literary tradition, format and structure. Pope was a broad enough thinker to recognize the poets' need for style and grace and to suggest that they be given that courtesy by the critics. The critics needed to appreciate that they, in spite of their Enlightenment education, could learn something new about critiquing poetry.

Regardless of Pope's original intention or the literary scholars' subsequent interpretations, it is clear that a few centuries later we have turned Pope's original line into a disparaging observation that I believe is a "myth" worthy of debunking. In our quest to develop curious minds, we should teach ourselves to be innovative, break the law of average, and become extraordinary. We should strive to become what the 16th century Italians called the "Renaissance Man" or in our case "man" or "woman." The Renaissance man or woman is one who is good at many things and seeks to develop skills in a variety of areas and subjects. Michelangelo and Leonardo da Vinci are two examples of the original Renaissance men, but history is strewn with others who embodied the principles to which the early Italians lay claim. For example, there is Benjamin Franklin, Thomas Jefferson, Bill Gates, Jimmy Carter, and even Brian May, guitarist for the band Queen, who was working on a PhD in astrophysics when the band began.[55]

People like these and others are not necessarily experts at anything, but they know more than just a little about "a lot of things," rather than being experts in one small silo of knowledge. I am not suggesting that you abandon your career as a lawyer, an actuary, or an accountant where you are bone-deep as a subject-matter expert in that particular field. Rather, I am suggesting that you be open to the prospect of getting a diverse and broad education, albeit an informal one, that will put you in the enviable position of being able to carry on discussions around a myriad of topics that are totally unrelated to your field of expertise. Your broad intellectual learning, even if it is "a little learning," will make you look different than the other accountants or actuaries you know. You will be able to stand out as if you are wearing "red" in a sea of "tan" suits.

In addition to the benefits of becoming a better intellectual conversationalist, there is a more practical reason for this broad, "little learning" education. Years ago, as a Partner at PwC, I learned a shocking fact. I discovered that the CEOs of my clients did not care one bit about generally accepted accounting principles, and had no interest in discussing them with me. So to get inside the so-called C-Suite, I had to be able to talk about subjects in which they were interested, such as access to the capital markets, outsourcing, or the geopolitical landscape in Europe. I had to invest in a "talking points" education that was way beyond my accounting expertise.

Similarly, I learned that the staff accountants that worked for me, and on whom I depended, had absolutely no knowledge of, or interest in, the music to which I listened. They would have been clueless if I had asked them to discuss the Platters, the Everly Brothers, or even Aretha Franklin, if you can imagine that! So, if I was going to relate to twenty-somethings, I had to invest in a "talking points" education on their music, e.g., Puddle of Mudd, 3 Doors Down, and A Flock of Seagulls. Did I need to become an expert in their music? Absolutely not! But by listening to the "Top 40" radio station every morning on the way to work, I had a basis for relating to people who I needed to work extraordinary hours for me. Occasionally, I would even let them catch me singing Eminem's "Cleanin' Out My Closet" or "Sk8er Boi" by Avril Lavigne just for fun.

My point is simply this. You need to embrace a diversity of

subjects that will allow you to better relate to both superiors and subordinates who may not always live in your accounting, legal, or business world. And it might just make you a more interesting person at your company's annual holiday party. Sometimes, a little learning is not a dangerous thing; it can be a lifesaver. So, contrary to your focused and targeted training as a professional, a marketing executive, a salesman, an accountant, a lawyer, or whatever your job or profession is, I want you to become a "deliberate dabbler." By that I mean someone who intentionally seeks knowledge outside their normal routine in a variety of areas. The subjects you choose to study or learn about do not matter. What does matter is that you broaden your knowledge of the world and develop a "talking points" education.

There are three important reasons I believe deliberate dabbling is important if you want to separate yourself from other people and become extraordinary.

**First, deliberate dabbling will help you identify and get in touch with those things that you are passionate about—** Remember, we are at our best when we find that convergence of our God-given talents, our learned skills, and our passions. You may recall the scene in the movie *Dead Poets Society* where the English teacher played by Robin Williams explains to his class why poetry is important. He says, "We don't read and write poetry because it's cute. We read and write poetry because we are members of the human race, and the human race is filled with passion. And medicine, law, business, engineering, these are noble pursuits and necessary to sustain life. But poetry, beauty, romance, love, these are what we stay alive for."[56] Hopefully, you can find your passion and pursue it relentlessly.

**Second, deliberate dabbling will result in or identify "knowledge gaps" that will entice and seduce you into a love affair with lifelong learning**—While Alexander Pope clearly refers to this idea in his "Essay on Criticism," a more practical reason is that scientists have determined we are more likely to learn new things when we have developed a little knowledge that serves to demonstrate just how little we know. In other words, the more we learn, the more we realize how little we know and the more we are encouraged to expand our knowledge even further.

**Finally, deliberate dabbling will help you communicate with people who are different than you**—Every person on the face of the planet is unique and therefore, different than you. I like to illustrate this point by asking students to take a sheet of notebook paper and tear it in half. Then I ask, "What are the odds of you taking a second sheet of paper and making the exact same tear you did the first time?" The answer, of course, is that it is virtually impossible to do. Similarly, you are constantly interfacing with people who are very different than you. They were raised in different cultures, have lived in different geographies and different economic conditions, have different educations, and have a completely different view of things like music, food, drink, hobbies, etc. But, you must communicate with all of these people at your job, your church or synagogue, and in your community. Some of them are your boss, your subordinate, your supplier, or your customer. Deliberate dabbling will help you build a vocabulary and a "little learning" knowledge base that will help you not only communicate, but perhaps establish relationships with people who are different from you.

Let me give you three exercises or assignments that will help you become a deliberate dabbler and, over time, realize the three objectives we have set out. These exercises can be used one at a time, or they can be used in concert with the same person or group of people.

## 1. Invest in a "talking points" or "little learning" education

In this exercise, I want you to identify a friend or associate that is a semi-official expert in some subject. Simply said, that means they know a whole lot more about the subject than you do. You can even practice this exercise with your spouse if you are brave enough. Over a period of a few weeks, I want you to deliberately research the topic and develop a "talking points" education that will allow you to carry on a conversation with your friend or associate. You don't need to become an expert. You just need to learn enough to understand the topic and the attendant circumstances that surround it.

Your objective is threefold. First, you want to understand the vocabulary of the topic. If it were baseball for example, you would want to know what an RBI is, the difference between a curve and a slider, and similar bits of information that are required to effectively communicate about the game. If the subject was the Middle East, you would want your research to show the borders of each country and the cultural differences between each country's people. Again, you're only seeking just enough of a vocabulary for you to carry on a conversation.

The second objective is for your "little learning" to be sufficient for you to be able to ask intelligent questions. Intelligent questions will keep you engaged in the discussion and will telegraph to your friend or associate that you are really interested in their topic.

Finally, your "talking points" education will hopefully be enough for you to occasionally contribute a meaningful thought or point to the discussion.

After the interaction with your friend or associate, reflect on what you learned both in your limited research and in the discussion and related feedback. How did it effect your relationship with your friend? Did the research and discussion pique your interest in learning more about the subject?

Did it identify a "knowledge gap" that enticed you to learn more about the topic? Did it perhaps light a spark that could eventually flame into full-blown passion? Don't panic if you answered no to all of these questions; this is a journey toward broadening your knowledge in a variety of topics. Not all of them will fascinate you, but maybe, one day, one of them just might have you climbing one mountain after another, seeking information to satiate your growing appetite.

## 2. Turn your ignorance into an asset

I often tell my students there is absolutely nothing wrong with ignorance. Ignorance is simply the absence of knowledge and we are all ignorant at some level. There is a lot wrong with "stupid," but stupid has nothing to do with ignorance. In this exercise, I want you to identify someone you know who has extensive knowledge in a subject in which you self-proclaim a reasonable level of ignorance. It may be some aspect of local history, the most recent scandalous murder trial, local politics and an upcoming election, the difference between hedge funds and private equity, or any similar personal or business topic. Engage them in a discussion and let them see how ignorant you are of that topic, but how interested you are in learning from them. After they have regaled you with their knowledge, reflect on what you have accomplished both for yourself and the other person.

Let me give you a real-life example of how this can work for you. Several years ago, I was working with GE Energy, a large subsidiary of GE Corporation, on a significant transaction in Houston, Texas. The financial leader of the deal was British and he considered himself a serious wine connoisseur. One night, at a very expensive restaurant in Houston, we were looking, with wonder, at the wine list and the substantial number of five-thousand-dollar bottles of wine on the list. But what really had my attention was the French wine that was listed for fifty-thousand-dollars. This provided a perfect opportunity to engage in a discussion with this very important GE executive around a subject about which I have limited and superficial knowledge, at best. So, in grand fashion, I decided to turn my ignorance into an asset. I expressed my amazement at such an expensive bottle of wine and confessed that I was clueless as to the vast differences in taste, quality, and price of French, Italian, German, Californian, Australian, and other wines. I asked the executive if he could really tell the difference between a three-hundred-dollar bottle of wine and a fifty-dollar bottle. Immediately, this energy executive and financial man became a teacher and wine tutor. Over the next two hours, my team and I received an education in vineyards, wineries, soil, sauvignons, chardonnays, Spanish reds, aging, and any number of other wine related topics. The executive genuinely enjoyed educating a country boy from Georgia, and as importantly, showing my team how much he really knew about the fruit of the vine. I decided to add a bit of intrigue to our discussion to ensure that I could continue developing a relationship with this executive. I allowed as to how we produced wine in the State of Georgia, and that I would be pleased to send him several bottles if he would taste and evaluate them against his basic French wine. Upon my return from the trip, I did indeed buy several bottles of wine from a vineyard in Tiger, Georgia, and sent them to Houston. After a few weeks, I received a detailed report that will remain unpublished in an effort to protect the innocence and reputation of all Georgia winemakers. The point of the story is that your ignorance can become an asset if you allow another person to express their knowledge. You not only learn, but you provide a venue for someone else to look and feel important. That is the essence of communication, and sometimes ignorance is bliss!

### 3. Become a shape-shifter

In the 2000 Marvel Comics film X-Men, the fictional character Mystique is a mutant with the ability of shape-shifting, being able to turn into anyone. Mystique assumes all physical attributes of those she is mimicking including taking on their fingerprints and retinal patterns. She even has the ability to shift her vocal cords to match their voice. She is a brilliant tactician and strategist. Aspiring leaders learn early that "shape-shifting", metaphorically speaking of course, is an essential tool in their journey to Extraordinary. The ability to slide in and out of roles seamlessly gives the aspiring leader a chance to get inside the head of another person; to understand their perspective, to relate to them and understand how they think. So what do I mean by shape-shifting or slipping and sliding in and out of roles? Let me explain. Each of us has a personality that is unique in the mathematical sense of "one and only one." It has been developed and cultivated over time by heredity and environment with innumerable contributing factors including, to name a few, our parents, our grandparents, our lifestyle, and our education. Consequently, we are all distinct from each other. You and I may differ because of the personalities of our great grandmothers on our fathers' side, or because you actually read Silas Marner in the sixth grade and I opted for an easier book, or because you spent your summers taking piano lessons while I was obsessed with baseball. Our heredity and environment, coupled with our intelligence and education, have defined who we are and the roles we play. Our different roles mean we have different interests, different passions, different skill sets, different friends, different jobs, different lifestyles and different perspectives. But our different roles do not mean that we cannot establish meaningful and productive relationships with each other. The leader who aspires to be extraordinary will embrace these differences and let them work to his or her advantage by becoming a "shape-shifter." Let's get specific. Imagine that you are the sales manager courting a potential customer with the prospect of bringing several million dollars of business to your company. You have met the customer's buyer a few times, but unfortunately, the two of you are seemingly worlds apart. You have been hesitating to push a business relationship because of your personality differences. You love NASCAR and country music and drink Budweiser, while he plays golf, is a season ticket holder to the opera and prefers French wines. How do you bridge what appears to be a wide and unfathomable gap? First, let's agree that I have no intention of changing, even if I could, either you or your potential customer's personality. Rather, I want to teach you, in three simple steps, how to become a shape-shifter. That's right; how to slip into a role that may not be permanently who you are, but a role that will let you get in the head, and maybe the pocketbook, of the potential customer.

- **Embrace your differences as an asset**—The tendency for most of us is to see our differences as a hurdle or an obstacle, and that simple mindset means we are, from the very beginning, facing an uphill climb. Rather than trying to navigate around our self-imposed obstacles, why not attack them head-on. Find the common ground between country music and opera; perhaps a discussion of the Opera Remix Initiative that began in 2011 bringing pop music and opera together. A little effort will reveal areas of commonality and will stimulate a lively discussion. Do your homework on the opera and slip into a role that gives you a guest pass into another world.

- **Become an active listener**—The best way to demonstrate your interest in a subject for which you have no affection is to be a proactive listener to someone who is passionate about the subject. Slip into the role of student and listen intently to the person talking; then start asking questions. You will, no doubt, learn something you did not know, but more importantly, you will send a clear message that you are willing to bridge the gap between their knowledge and yours.

- **Follow through**—Don't let the discussion end with your initial meeting. Send a note recounting the topics you discussed or a published article that is relevant and on point. Remember, your objective is to get inside the head of the person and demonstrate that you are interested in understanding more about them. And in doing so, you might just build a walkway across a chasm of differences that originally seemed impossible to overcome.

## The Journey to Extraordinary: Tips for the Traveler...

Take a sheet of plain notebook paper and tear it into two pieces. Now imagine the probability of making that exact same tear again. That is precisely how unique you and I are as individuals. Search for and embrace the differences of your fellow travelers on the journey to Extraordinary. They may help you get there faster, and unquestionably, they will make the trip more interesting.

# CHAPTER 5

# You Can't Judge a Book by Its Cover

## Maximize your First Encounters

The frequently used saying, "You can't judge a book by its cover," certainly implies the very positive idea that we should be careful in rushing to judgment on a book, an object, or even a person without doing the proper diligence or investigation to determine if the inner workings are reflective of its outer shell or cover. Unlike most of the myths we examine in this book, this one is relatively new having first been used circa 1944 in an edition of the African journal, *American Speech*, which used the quote, "You can't judge a book by its binding." Apparently, the idiom grew in popularity when it appeared in the novel, *Murder in the Glass Room*, by Lester Fuller and Edwin Rolfe (1946) although it was changed slightly to "You can never tell a book by its cover."[57]

Notwithstanding the altruistic intent of the saying, nor a judgment that it is not quite ancient enough to qualify as a "myth," the fact remains that it is just not true. You can, indeed, "judge a book by its cover" and you prove it every day. When you see a person walking down the street dressed in black from head to toe, their hair dyed blood red, tattoos of the Grim Reaper and the numerals 666 on each arm, piercings in both ears and through their nose and upper lip, and wearing hobnail boots covered in chains, you make a quick judgment about the person and your interest in sharing coffee or having a relationship with them. The question is not whether we should or should not judge a book by its cover; that's a debate I will leave with you and your ethical conscience. The fact remains that human nature forces us to make judgments about the things and people we see based on our individual backgrounds and our perceptions of the situation at hand.

For example, you might not think twice about our "Frankenstein-looking" character described above if you were walking into a Halloween costume party. On the other hand, you would likely be horrified if you were exiting the elevator in your office building or worse if you were about to close the door of your car in the office parking garage. Appearances matter! But lest you think I have exaggerated with a preposterous example, let's consider a more subtle and modest thought. Every day of the year, thousands, if not millions, of businesspeople go to their offices wearing outfits that literally push the limits of "business casual" right to the edge. This deformalization of business dress that began in the mid-1990s has continued for almost twenty-five years and has reached the point where America's workforce has a homogeneous look on the business dress spectrum somewhere between country club relaxed and canoe casual.

While relaxation of corporate dress codes has generally had a positive influence on the work environment—we have learned that we can think just as well without neckties or pantyhose—in our continuing quest to become extraordinary, Homogeneous is the first cousin to Average. We wear our khaki pants, polo shirts, and Toms shoes, sit in our cubicles, and look just like everyone else. You may be the smartest, most creative person in the group, but the first appearance suggests that you are like everyone else. When I was a kid, my childhood hero was the Lone Ranger, and even then, I always wondered why the Ranger wore a baby blue outfit and a white hat when all the other cowboys in the TV shows were dressed in dull browns and greys. It was an intentional exaggeration to say that this guy is different. It had nothing to do with how well he handled a six-gun, or how adept he was at riding a horse, or if he was a good guy with deep moral convictions. It was all about the appearance that told the viewers this guy is different than the rest; so, pay attention. The Ranger's outfit caused us to "judge the book by its cover" before we experienced a single episode.

Hopefully, business associates, customers, clients, and others will recognize that they really shouldn't judge a book by its cover, and take time to understand the depth that lies beyond that first monochromatic impression they have of us. Unfortunately, the frenzied pace of commerce suggests otherwise. I have probably read a hundred serious resumes a year from people looking for a new job. I throw out at least 75% of them after a first reading because they are either poorly written, poorly organized, or otherwise do nothing to catch my attention and convince me there is something there beyond the Average. Similarly, e-book publishers tell the same story. Most manuscripts they receive are rejected out of hand without being read because the proposed cover of the book is bland or otherwise not different enough to pull it out of the average category. Who knows, maybe the next Fortune 500 CFO or CEO lies in the bowels of my average-looking resumes. Perhaps the average book covers hide the next John Milton or Ernest Hemingway. Unfortunately, they linger in obscurity because appearance and first impressions really do matter.

The good news is that appearance and first impressions are totally under your control. You have control over every first impression you make, every first paragraph you write, every word you speak, and every question you ask. You can turn the old myth, "you can't judge a book by its cover," and the human nature that invariably does the opposite and renders judgment, into an asset that works to your advantage.

Let me suggest seven proactive steps that, when taken in concert, will guarantee that your appearance and first impression will get attention and will lead your underlying substance from obscurity to Extraordinary.

## 1. Establish your own personal style of dress

This is your own approach to business dress. If you are a man, start with wool pants and cotton (non-polo) shirts. Mix in a blazer and tie at least one day a week, and surprise them periodically with a suit and a crisp white shirt. Women should consider a combination of fashionable business suits with a mix of dressy slacks and button-down shirts or blouses. You are creating an optical reputation internally and externally that makes a statement about who you are and how serious you are about your job. In effect, you are saying to those around you, "Take a good look at the cover of this book because you can judge me by my appearance and what you find on the inside is even better than the cover suggests." In middle Georgia where I come from, the old saying was, "He or she is like a Vidalia onion; the more you peel, the sweeter they get."

I am not suggesting that you go back to the early 1990s when everyone was expected to wear a tie every day. Embrace business casual and make it your own, but create your own style that sets you apart from the polo shirt and khaki pants crowd. The best advice I can give you is to strive to consistently dress at least one level above your peers.

I understand the pushback surrounding this topic suggesting that today's business environment has changed, doesn't require anyone to play dress-up, and that it is generally accepted to go to work in uber-casual wear. But I want you to remember, I am not asking you to fit in with the crowd; and I am not suggesting that you blend in with the homogenous group that is satisfied with Average. I am suggesting that you break the current unwritten rules that dictate informal dress every day and create a presence and appearance that is consistent with your journey to become Extraordinary.

Three very positive things happen when you find your own style of dress with which you are comfortable:

**First, you will have a more positive attitude about yourself**—When you look good, you feel good, and your attitude will become contagious. People around you will recognize that you are just a little different, and they will be inspired by the confidence they see in you.

**Second, a consistent style and confident appearance will help you stay externally driven, rather than internally focused**—Whether you are an accountant, lawyer, businesswoman, manager, or other professional, if you want to become Extraordinary you eventually have to focus on the customer and on generating revenues and profits for your company. There are, of course, exceptions to this rule. If your competency is above average, or you are extremely technical in your field, you may very well be able to achieve great success, and even become Extraordinary, by keeping your head down in your office and ignoring all else around you.

These situations, I might add, are rare. At PwC, we had technicians that were much smarter than everyone else; we really tried to keep them internally focused since that was their "highest and best use." I often joked that we kept those people in a dark room in New York City and threw red meat to them at least once a day. For most of us who are not so cerebrally blessed, it is important that we stay externally driven and market-focused. A well-groomed, confident and consistent appearance will help ensure that you stand out in a crowd.

**Finally, a confident appearance will make you more comfortable in meeting new people, both inside and outside your organization, and will lead to relationships that will be extremely beneficial as you grow personally, corporately, and financially.**

A trio of parting comments is worth considering as you create your consistent style. First, polish your shoes once a week. It is amazing how many people would never think of wearing a dirty shirt to work, but they will wear scuffed and dirty shoes without a second thought. Notice that in order to polish your shoes, they must have a bit of leather in them. This advice is equally important for men and women. And second, always buy clothes that fit. Ill-fitting clothes say more about you than you can imagine. Enough said. Finally, avoid what I call "canoe casual." Over the last several years, I have seen staff members wearing cotton trousers that have never experienced a crease, shirts with no collars, and shoes without an ounce of leather. I finally decided counseling was necessary when one of my partners, who should have known better, came to the office in what I could only define as camping attire. I dubbed him "canoe casual," and suggested that a few pairs of wool pants, shirts with collars, and leather shoes, might make him a little more presentable. He listened, and today is an extraordinary partner and leader.

## 2. Surprise people by breaking expectations

If you want to make a great impression on your boss, a subordinate, your spouse or significant other, your customer, or literally anyone you meet, simply surprise them. The easiest way to do that is to exceed their expectations. Exceeding people's expectations is usually not hard since most of us are programmed to expect and live with Average. For example, when you are in a remote location and get a cup of coffee out of a vending machine, you are generally happy with it, even if the coffee's two best qualities are hot and wet, because your expectations were so low. In our homogeneous work environment, we learn to expect and appreciate Average. In fact

Average is contagious. If you are not careful, when you are in an environment where Average is the norm, you adapt and find that you are delivering just what someone expects. This dilemma is the reason there is culture shock in an organization when a new CEO comes in and changes the cadence and culture of the business. Suddenly, the norm has changed, the bar is raised, and expectations become significantly elevated.

If you want to become Extraordinary then become the influence that breaks the existing expectations for your company and for the people around you. Surprise them! Let me give you three suggestions that are guaranteed to break expectations and create an impression that will be more welcome than a shining beacon on a foggy night.

- **Go overboard in preparation**—In every assignment or project, find a way to go at least just beyond what you believe is expected. Average people deliver "as expected." Extraordinary people find a way to deliver just a little more.

- **Always show up, show up on time, and show up dressed to play**—If you accomplish these three seemingly obvious and simple goals, you will create an impression that is demonstrably different that most of the people around you. I am amazed at how many times I go to a business meeting where several people straggle in late because of traffic jams, where they did not bother to bring the materials to be discussed, and worse than all, where they have not read the materials in advance. I frequently turn to the people who are unprepared and say, "Would a preacher go to church without his Bible? Would a carpenter go to work without his hammer?" Finally, the meeting starts, but the impressions have been made and I have proved that our old saying, "You can't judge a book by its cover," really is a myth because everyone in the room has made judgments about the tardy and unprepared participants without a shred of evidence of their intelligence, competence, or integrity. Surprise people. Show up, show up on time, and show up dressed to play.

- **Add a personal touch that is uniquely you**—In a world where email and texting have become the standard and ubiquitous forms of communications, a personal touch stands out and differentiates you from all the rest. There are so many little things you can do to make a lasting impression. For example, buy personal stationary and make a habit of sending short, handwritten notes to people with whom you have met. I promise you they will not be expecting it and they will remember you for your thoughtfulness. The added benefit is that a handwritten note sends a message that you think that person is important enough for you to take the time to put the words on paper, buy a stamp, and mail it. Similarly, small, inexpensive gifts make a huge impression on people. Anything you do that demonstrates you cared enough to do it becomes memorable to the recipient. The most significant reason for this is that in a world of Average the little effort you make is usually totally unexpected and your slight effort becomes Extraordinary.

There are literally dozens of thoughtful gestures you can make that will surprise people. Experiment and find a few that can become the unique expression of who you are. Surprise people and let them "judge your book cover." They will be even more surprised when they peel the onion and find that you only get sweeter and sweeter.

### 3. Learn the art of the impactful paragraph

Hopefully, we have established that people do indeed judge you by the first impression you make. Perhaps we should all be more patient and "judge the tree by the fruit it bears," but, realistically, we all have a hair trigger on our judging mechanisms and appearances, and first impressions do matter. This is not only true with our outward, nonverbal appearance but also with the words we speak and the words we write.

My experience in teaching undergraduates and business school graduate students is that most of them leave their respective universities, at best, as average writers and, more commonly, as awful writers. When they arrive at work, they are shocked at how much they actually have to write and the importance of efficient communications.

Extraordinary people learn early the art of the impactful

paragraph—the ability to capture the attention of their reader quickly and to entice them into reading more. While there is an art to this process, it does not require drama or attention-grabbing gimmicks. In fact, the techniques are unusually simple and easy to learn. It starts with the basic principle that busy people have no time to browse through eloquent prose in search of the main point like they are on an Easter egg hunt searching for the prize egg. They want to understand the issues, the relevant facts, alternatives available, and a path forward.

The following simple techniques, focused on writing a simple paragraph, will help you communicate more efficiently and effectively in writing and persuade your reader to agree with the proposed solution or conclusions.

- **Start with a single subject or idea and one purpose—** This allows everything you write to build and support that purpose. It should begin with a short introduction or topic sentence followed by supporting facts, and end with a clear conclusion or transition to the next paragraph. Remember, you are telling a story with one controlling idea, albeit a very short one.

- **Always use the active rather than the passive voice—**The active voice is more authoritative and makes the reader focus on actions that need to be taken.

- **Use summarization techniques to help organize your thoughts or points**—Bullet points are effective in helping focus the reader's attention on your purpose.

- **Create a flow that is easy to read and follow**—Proper transition words and phrases like consequently, therefore, notwithstanding, furthermore, nevertheless, etc. all serve to keep bringing the reader's attention back to your controlling idea.

- **Finally, proofread the paragraph**—The fastest way to lose a reader is to allow them to magnify the extremes by focusing on misspelled words, typos, improper punctuation, sentence fragments, or stumbling over misplaced gerunds, split infinitives, and all the other unpardonable sins you learned about in elementary school.

### 4. Learn to speak for five minutes with clarity and alacrity

Five minutes does not seem like a long time, but my students cringe at the thought of having to deliver a five-minute presentation on a complicated topic. History would differ on that view, however, and suggests that five minutes is plenty of time to deliver a meaningful and influential talk. Consider the following examples that are the courtesy of Darrell Zahorsky and George Matthew Adams:

- Napoleon wrote that the reason he beat the Austrians was that they did not know the value of five minutes.
- It took Abraham Lincoln less than five minutes to deliver his immortal Gettysburg Address.
- In less than five minutes, William Jennings Bryan electrified a political convention with a single expression in his "Cross of Gold" speech that gave him the nomination for the presidency of the United States.

The key in making a five-minute presentation, whether formal or informal, is to make every minute of the five organized and deliberate. Let me give you five specific actions you can take to make your short presentations provocative/thought-provoking.

- Know your material "cold." Go overboard in research and preparation.
- Organize your thoughts in segments that cover the "screaming" headlines. This will help you prioritize the most important points.
- Get the attention of your audience early. Start with a provocative/thought-provoking comment or observation that gets their attention and alerts them that the really good stuff is coming.
- Make sure you tell a story. There should be a flow and rhythm to your remarks that build from the introduction to the conclusion.

- Practice, Practice and Practice. You will get better and better and feel more at ease if you have tested your words against a clock.

## 5. Learn to write a functional resume and a cover letter

Everybody needs to know how to write an effective functional resume whether you are currently employed or still looking for a job. I advise young people that I mentor to prepare your resume and update it at least quarterly. The magic is in preparing a resume that does not necessarily focus on the chronology of your education or job history, but rather the functional skills that the prospective employer is seeking.

I have hired hundreds of staff accountants and investment bankers over the years and I have concluded that there are four major functional skills on which all prospective employers are focused. First, can the prospect think three-dimensionally? In other words, can they deal with concepts that need to be developed into ideas or are they limited by their inability to escape linear thinking. Second, is the prospect comfortable in having a ten-minute conversation in which they demonstrate an ability to listen, process, and then ask questions? Third, can the prospect write reasonably well? Can they string ten sentences together in a paragraph that is logical and flows from introduction to conclusion? Finally, does the prospect have demonstrable experience in working in a team environment?

These four elements are the pillars around which a functional resume should be built. University and business school education, prior work experience, and social and community involvement provide substantial data that can be organized around these fundamentals. Don't sell yourself short; you may have limited actual job experience but ample experience to demonstrate the four pillars. The resume should be truthful and answer several questions even before an employer asks them: How much analytical ability does he or she have? Has this person been in a role where they had to solve problems? Has this person led a team before and are they comfortable in an environment where success is dependent not on individual performance, but teamwork?

This functional resume is designed to stand out amongst the hundreds of average resumes that an employer will read. A well-written functional resume has a much better chance of getting an employer's attention than a chronological one. An added touch is to write a cover letter that focuses specifically on the job you are considering and the skills you know the employer will value. The letter should be no longer than one page and should have bold and clear points that demonstrate a clear vision of your career goals, the skills that are relevant to the job, and why you think you can create value for the employer. A well-written cover letter almost always ensures that your resume gets read and most likely results in a personal interview. Simply extraordinary!

CURIOSITY ~~KILLED~~ THE CAT
<br>made

## 6. Develop confidence with the "Rule of Three."

The Rule of Three is not a new concept. It has been around since the time of Aristotle, and has certainly been a major part of English literature for a few hundred years. The concept is simply that people tend to remember things if they are presented in groups of three. Think about it. There were three musketeers, three blind mice, three Billy Goats Gruff, and three bears in the Goldilocks story.

Great political speeches have always relied on the Rule of Three. Remember these? 1) "Friends, Romans, and Countrymen" (William Shakespeare); 2) "Blood, sweat, and tears" (General George Patton); and 3) "Our priorities are education, education, and education" (Prime Minister Tony Blair). In fact, the Rule of Three has become far-reaching in our past and present language. We teach our kids to "stop, look, and listen," we govern based on "life, liberty, and the pursuit of happiness," we watch "the good, the bad, and the ugly," and we worship "the Father, the Son, and the Holy Ghost." From Julius Caesar, who said, "Veni, vidi, vici (I came, I saw, I conquered)" to "Bah, bah, black sheep, have you any wool? Yes sir, yes sir, three bags full," we all learned via the Rule of Three. The amazing thing, however, is that very few of us, whether in a business environment or a casual setting, know how to evoke the Rule of Three to our advantage.

Several years ago, it dawned on me that there was rarely an oral presentation I had to make, a solution I had to offer, a problem I had to solve, or a response I had to give that I could not boil down to three major points. And when I realized the impact the Rule of Three had on my audience or listener, I became a master at applying it to every major discussion I had. Here is what I learned. Every time, and I do mean every time, I am asked a question such as "How do you think we should respond to the offer price," my answer is always, "I think there are three things we should do." Immediately, three things happen. First, my client's ears perk up because I have alerted him or her that I am about to give them a preformulated list. Second, I watch them reach for a pen because I have put them on notice that this will not be a long list, and they can easily keep track for future reference. And finally, I watch as they review the list and then begin to discuss each point in more detail. Then I know I have not just captured their imagination by an oratorical trick of the threes, but that I have engaged them intellectually in considering the three points.

One of the most effective uses for the Rule of Three is to invoke it well before someone asks you a question that requires a response. Learn to finish your thoughts on a subject being discussed by saying, "Let me summarize where I am on this with three thoughts."

Effective use of the Rule of Three is a learned skill. I do not have a photographic memory, and I am no smarter than you. I taught myself how to implement the Rule of Three at will, and in any situation, the old-fashioned way: Practice, Practice,

Practice. In my own personal and professional network, I am now renowned for my seemingly amazing ability to capture any series of complicated issues or thoughts in three simple elements. Such was not always the case. When I first decided that I could make this simple rule work for me, I practiced every chance I could—often under friendly fire. Sometimes, I would get through two points and go blank. More often, I would have to default to four or five points. Over time, I developed a process that is now intuitive for me. The majority of the time when I am asked a question, serious business or even casual, I immediately begin to focus my thoughts toward three things.

Let me give you three simple steps you can practice that will help you master this invaluable tool. But, at the outset, you need to commit to consciously looking for opportunities to invoke the Rule of Three.

- **Narrow the issues down quickly to the biggest or most important ones**—This will force you to naturally prioritize your thoughts and eliminate "noise" around the real issues.
- **Use the active, rather than the passive, voice, and phrase your points as actionable items if possible**—The active voice is much more authoritative, and action items automatically invite the listener to become a party to the tasks being suggested.
- **Seek immediate feedback on your three points**—I always put my three points out there, and then ask a direct ques-

tion designed to get either confirmation or a different view. For me it's easy to just say, "Do you think that works?" or "Does that make sense?" Seeking immediate feedback will give you a sanity check on what you said, and ensure you are getting buy-in for later actions.

Whether explaining why you shot 89 rather than 80 on the golf course, explaining your view of national healthcare, or recommending solutions to problems at work, look for opportunities to use the Rule of Three. If you practice these techniques a few times, you will find that the process becomes easier and easier and you will get better and better at your execution.

Remember, we were all trained as children to learn and visualize in groups of three. When you find an opportunity to use The Rule of Three, remember the three little pigs and the three blind mice and you will know your audience is ready for you.

## 7. Develop an attitude of resilience

Extraordinary people have a way of bouncing back from adversity or failure; they are resilient. Psychologists have done substantial work around the study of resilience in an effort to determine why some people are resilient and can bounce back from difficulty and others never recover. While the research is mixed as to how much resilience is genetically based—clearly some people are naturally more resilient than others—there is general agreement on the characteristics that resilient people possess and some sense that training can teach people to better respond to failures or great difficulties. Resilient people tend to possess or reflect the following characteristics:

- **Positive Attitude**—This does not mean just a spirit of optimism. In fact, often times, optimism in adverse circumstances can mean disaster. Jim Collins, who happened upon this concept while researching *Good to Great*, his book on how companies transform themselves out of mediocrity, had a hunch (an exactly wrong hunch) that resilient companies were filled with optimistic people. He tried out that idea on Admiral Jim Stockdale, who was held prisoner and tortured by the Vietcong for over seven years. Collins recalls:

  > I asked Stockdale, "Who didn't make it out of the camps?" and he said, "Oh, that's easy. It was the optimists. They were the ones who said we were going to be out by Christmas. And then they said we'd be out by Easter and then out by Fourth of July and out by Thanksgiving, and then it was Christmas again." Then Stockdale turned to me and said, "You know, I think they all died of broken hearts."[58]

  Resilient people don't see difficult circumstances through rose-colored glasses or with blind optimism. They tend to see them as challenges rather than insurmountable obstacles and their positive attitude allows them to see the cause of their angst and pain as temporary problems, rather than hopeless dilemmas. As a result, resilient people are able to retain control over the emotions that would frustrate or severely depress others.

- **Grounded Sense of Reality**—Resilient people have a fundamental understanding of—and are grounded in—reality. They are somehow able to take a clinical view of their failures and recognize that they are not immune to problems, but simply have to deal with them. They reflect the attitude that Rudyard Kipling no doubt had in mind when he penned the lines "If you can meet with Triumph and Disaster and treat those two impostors just the same."

- **Refusal to Become a Victim**—Over the years I have watched innumerable people who had a significant failure, or faced a significant problem, immediately adopt a "victim status." They became victims of organizational change, new policies, bad timing, office politics, and any number of other excuses for their failures. The "victim" will likely want to play a game that I call "Oh, ain't it awful!"—"Oh, ain't it awful that my bonus is down this year;" "Oh, ain't it awful that I have been mistreated in the compensation plan." This actually can be a very fun game to play because

it places all the blame squarely on the shoulders of someone else. It even becomes more fun when you can arrange
for two or more others to play the game with you. The "Oh,
ain't it awfuls" become exponentially more commiserative
and more fun. Resilient people refuse to allow themselves
to become victims. They recognize that victims become
self-focused and obsessed with their failure. Victims relin-
quish control of their emotions to an invisible alter ego.
And victims become defensive and have little chance of
making positive contributions while they wallow in their
self-defeat.

- **Higher Meaning to Life**—Resilient people understand and
  appreciate that there is more to life than the job they hold,
  the position they are in, or their current income. These are
  all transient stations that might sustain us physically, and
  even emotionally, but they do not provide long-term meaning to our lives. Many psychologists agree that belief in "a
  greater meaning to life" is how resilient people find a path to
  the future when their current circumstances are so miserable. Diane Coutu, Director of Client Communications at
  Banyan Family Business Advisors, discussed this concept
  in her *Harvard Business Review* article, "How Resilience
  Works."[59] She explains that this concept (greater meaning to
  life theory) was beautifully articulated by Viktor E. Frankl,
  an Austrian psychiatrist and an Auschwitz survivor. In the

midst of staggering suffering, Frankl invented "meaning therapy," a humanistic therapy technique that helps individuals make the kinds of decisions that will create significance in their lives. In his book *Man's Search for Meaning*, Frankl described the pivotal moment in the camp when he developed meaning therapy. He was on his way to work one day, worrying whether he should trade his last cigarette for a bowl of soup. He wondered how he was going to work with a new foreman whom he knew to be particularly sadistic. Suddenly, he was disgusted by just how trivial and meaningless his life had become. He realized that to survive, he had to find some purpose. Frankl did so by imagining that he was giving a lecture after the war on the psychology of the concentration camp to help outsiders understand what he had been through. Although he wasn't even sure he would survive, Frankl created some concrete goals for himself. In doing so, he succeeded in rising above the sufferings of the moment. As he put it in his book: "We must never forget that we may also find meaning in life even when confronted with a hopeless situation, when facing a fate that cannot be changed."[60] Resilient people find faith in the future and that faith bridges the gap between their current disaster and failure to a more hopeful tomorrow.

Appearances do matter, whether they are physical, emotional, verbal or nonverbal. Extraordinary people pay attention to appearances and they deliberately find ways to break the back of Average. They are sensitive to the fact that people do, indeed, "judge their book by its cover," and they proactively look for ways to bias their judgment. They create an appearance and style that is unique to them, they surprise people by exceeding their expectations, they leave a lasting impression with their written and spoken word, and they bridge their failures of the past to the successes of the future with a resilient attitude.

## The Journey to Extraordinary: Tips for the Traveler...

First impressions are just not fair; they may be absolutely wrong and hence disguise the greatness that lies behind the mask of that first encounter. But it's worse; first impressions are not limited to our physical appearance, but also to our written and spoken words. Aspiring travelers on the road to Extraordinary learn to go overboard in preparation, find their own style of consistently tasteful dress and master the art of speaking with both clarity and alacrity. Remember, unfair or not, we all judge the book by looking at its cover.

# CHAPTER 6

# A Bird in the Hand is Worth Two in the Bush

## Grasp Opportunity

The origin of this old saying is uncertain but the earliest English version is from the Bible and was translated into English in John Wycliffe's version in 1382: Ecclesiastes IX—A living dog is better than a dead lion.[61] Circa 1450, the saying was found in John Capgrave's *The Life of Saint Katherine*: "It is more sekyr [certain] a byrd in your fest, than to haue three in the sky a-boue."[62] Other versions mentioning birds came later. The earliest of those is in Hugh Rhodes' *The Boke of Nurture or Schoole of Good Maners*, circa 1530: "A bird in hand—is worth ten flye at large."[63] Regardless of the origin, the concept is the same: you are better having a sure thing today than you are in taking a risk that you can have something better tomorrow.

This "bird in the hand" theory suggests, of course, that there is merit in being satisfied in your current position and in not being so greedy as to always want more, or risk losing everything you have in the pursuit of more. And who can argue with this noble thought? One can imagine Benjamin Franklin walking the streets of Philadelphia saying, "A penny saved is a penny earned!" But this thought process—"a bird in the hand is worth two in the bush" and "a penny saved is a penny earned"—is, at the risk of offending one of our founding fathers, the thought process of Average. Extraordinary people are not shackled by the need to protect what they have, but continuously inspired by the vision of how much more the future can bring. They are not willing to settle for what is "in hand," whether it is a mediocre job, a good performance report, a tried and true process, or the next satisfactory outcome. They see an exploding career that exceeds expectations, innovation that renders tried and true as tired and timid, and ever-improving results that make satisfactory outcomes seem as old and quaint as dial-up internet. In short, extraordinary people are never satisfied with a "bird in the hand," and therein lies the myth.

The old idiom should have been restated a long time ago to propose that, "a bird in the hand of the Average man is worth two in the bush." In fact, for over two hundred years, ordinary people in every generation have proven that they can, with the combination of vision, hard work, and courage, turn the ordinary into extraordinary, make the impossible seem routine and bring the unimagined into a virtual reality. And this willingness to risk what is in hand to accomplish what the mind can imagine is not limited to the handful of unusually talented people we read about. It is not limited to Thomas Edison, Henry Ford, Nikola Tesla, or even the likes of Bill Gates. American business over the last one hundred years has been built by entrepreneurs, whether they are technology originators, healthcare innovators, small niche manufacturers or simply unemployed workers embracing a franchising opportunity like the local yogurt shop in your neighborhood.

It is these men and women who are willing to risk it all for a chance at independence and the success that drives the American economy. Men and women just like you who are not satisfied with Average, and are willing to take risks to go beyond that which is in hand and passionately pursue that which is elusive. Is the number of people who regularly debunk the myth that the "bird in the hand is worth two in the bush" limited to a select few who are born with a neurotic personality that allows them to be innately perennial risk-takers, or can ordinary men and women learn to become risk-takers as well? I believe the answer is overwhelmingly yes to the latter, but first we have to define the term "risk-taker."

The preponderance of scholarly literature explores risk as a behavioral characteristic most often affiliated with dangerous activities or negligent or near negligent behavior that can often become addictive. There is some suggestion that personality plays a role in a person's likelihood to take more risks, although the conclusions are mixed. Some studies indicate that people who score high (in personality tests) on neuroticism—a combination of anxiety, moodiness, and worry—are more likely to become risk-takers, while others conclude that risk-takers score lower on neuroticism tests than the general population. Notwithstanding that psychological studies tend to focus on the negative aspects of risk-taking, there is clear recognition of the positive impacts. In the article "The Psychology of Risk-Taking," Zawn Villines says, "While some risky behaviors might not be worth their potential consequences, risk-taking in small doses is almost universally beneficial for your brain and mental health. Novel experiences can help to ward off depression and reinvigorate a stale relationship. Risk-taking is often a necessary prerequisite for starting a new business or launching a new career, and the excitement associated with uncertainty can be a powerful antidote to boredom and even depression. Because dopamine produces a natural high, risk-taking behaviors can help you get a positive mood and a new perspective without the risks associated with drug use."[64]

The psychologists also report a significant correlation between the propensity for taking risks in adolescents and adults. Margo Gardner and Laurence Steinberg of Temple University, in their study, "Peer Influence on Risk Taking,

Risk Preference, and Risky Decision-making in Adolescence and Adulthood: An Experimental Study," stated that "Analyses indicated that (a) risk taking and risky decision-making decreased with age; (b) participants took more risks, focused more on the benefits than the costs of risky behavior, and made riskier decisions when in peer groups than alone; and (c) peer effects on risk taking and risky decision-making were stronger among adolescents and youths than adults."[65] The conclusions of this scientific study are interesting and provide insight into the reasons that people, especially those in business, have so easily succumbed to the old myth "A bird in the hand is worth two in the bush."

Two observations are worth noting. First, the older we become, the less likely we are to become risk-takers. Over time, concerns about safety and comfort diminish our enthusiasm and sense of adventure. We become highly focused on protecting what we have, or what we have achieved, and are unwilling to risk our current position to achieve more. As a result, we stay in our current jobs long after they have stopped being fun, we shelve our ambition to travel the world, we delay our decision to learn a new language, and we put off pursuit of our dreams until they fade into obscurity. The lesson is pretty clear; you are not getting any younger so don't wait. Act now.

Dr. Betty Siegel, former President of Kennesaw State University, told me the story of her husband, Joel, who at fifty-two years old decided that he wanted to go law school, but was afraid he was too old. His observation was that "When I get out of law school in three years, I will be fifty-five years old." Dr. Siegel's response: "Joel, if you choose not to go to law school, in three years you will be fifty-five anyway." Joel went to law school, and, until recently, was practicing as a Magistrate Court judge. The takeaway is that time will not wait on you. Don't hesitate. Pursue your dream now while you still can.

My personal story provides a similar lesson. I spent thirty-seven wonderful years with the international professional services firm, Price Waterhouse, now known as PwC. The truth, however, is that I really always wanted to be a teacher; unfortunately, I didn't think I could make enough money teaching school. When I retired at age 59, the Dean of the Business School at Kennesaw State University asked me to join the faculty and teach. I asked what course I could teach and he said, "Larry, whatever you want." After suggesting that I wanted to teach English literature, the Dean tactfully postured that I might not be qualified and suggested that I create a course where I was qualified. So I created a course in Mergers and Acquisitions that I would teach in the Masters of Business Administration program.

I have to tell you that this decision came with more than a little fear and trepidation. I had never done this before. I was a practitioner, and certainly not an academic or, as I like to say, a member of "the Academy." How would I handle graduate students? What if they started asking questions that I could not answer? How much embarrassment would I be able to handle? After the first day in the classroom, my fears surprisingly vanished. I realized what I had been missing for so many years. I loved the classroom. Do not wait as long as I did to pursue your dream. Do it now. Take the risk. The reward will be exponential in comparison to the risk you take.

The second observation from the aforementioned psychological research is that it is much easier to take risks when you have the protection of a group of people rather than when you are in the spotlight alone. When a group succeeds, the group gets the glory, and when the group fails the failure is shared by the group, and individual performance or nonperformance is secondary. But when you are acting alone, when the decision is yours and yours alone, the success or failure falls directly on you.

This fear of failure is strong and palpable and inhibits our willingness to take risks that leave us naked and exposed in the spotlight. You can see this fundamental group versus individual dynamic played out in teenagers who learn early on that there is safety in large numbers. They perceive less risk when they are acting as a class or a group. They party in large groups on spring break where individual behavior is lost in the larger group where "everyone is doing it." When taken to the extreme, you can also see this individual/group dynamic manifested in street gangs where individuals feel protected and are willing to take more risks as part of the gang than they would when acting by themselves.

Now translate that same dynamic—individual spotlight versus protection by the group—to the world of business, and you start getting closer to where you and I live. We are much more inclined to voice a complaint at work when we can do it as part of a group, even a smaller group. We are much more likely to suggest a risky proposal when we have the support of others who are willing to share the risks with us. The palpable fear of failure is, indeed, strong and grows stronger the farther away we get from our "protection."

Unfortunately, extraordinary success does not usually come to those who hunt in packs. If it does, however, an extraordinary individual is most likely leading the pack. Big accomplishments come to the individual who is willing to abandon the protection of the group and step in the arena by themselves. Extraordinary success comes to the individual who recognizes that a bird in the hand is not enough, and that there is so much more waiting in "the bush." Phenomenal results comes to the individual who is able to overcome the fear of failure, ignore the ridicule of embarrassment, and push past the procrastination that keeps them warm and safe in the blanket of group homogeneity. Extraordinary success comes to the courageous lone warrior.

But wait, you might say! Are you suggesting that in order

to be Extraordinary, I should just cavalierly plunge ahead without regard to the risks that could crater my journey at any moment? Certainly not! Ordinary people who achieve extraordinary results recognize the risks they face, but they learn how to manage the risks and even harness them to their advantage. Individuals who want to break from the safety of the group and Average, and begin a quest for the "two in the bush," need, in the words of the author Bill Treasurer, to "take their courage to work." Mr. Treasurer says in his book, *Courage Goes to Work*, that "The normal human response to fear is to hunker down and play it safe. But if everyone is playing it safe, a business is in real danger of missing significant opportunities. When you're anxious, worried, or scared and feel the urge to hunker down and play it safe, that's the time you need to do just the opposite. Playing it safe never leads to greatness. That's where courage comes in."[66] Or, in the words of a good friend of mine, "the Good Lord hates a coward!"

So in your quest for the "two in the bush," how do you develop the courage to break from the group and become Extraordinary? Perhaps you already have that courage deep inside and, like the Lion in *The Wizard of Oz*, you just need someone to help you bring it to the surface. Let me give you five specific steps and initiatives you can take that will help you harness your courage and exploit the risks in your quest for the "two in the bush."

## 1. Create a bias for action

If you want to go beyond Average, reach a specific goal, pursue a lifelong dream, become an expert in some subject, or generally achieve more than you have already, the most important step you can take is to START. That's right, just push the GO button! In theory it seems so simple. Just begin the process, start the journey, put your fingers on the keyboard or pick up your pen and write.

In practice, the act of starting proves exceedingly difficult for most people and often great ideas lay dormant, not for lack of genius, but for lack of initiative. Entrepreneurial spirit starts innately with a curious mind, but without a catalyst for action, the entrepreneur remains little more than a dreamer who wanders in the ethereal espousing lofty ideas that capture the imagination but evaporate before developing a footing that leads to traction and eventual success. Most of us have hundreds of good reasons why we haven't pushed that symbolic GO button—insufficient hours in the day, incomplete research, the need for additional inspiration, the lack of financial resources, and those elusive missing pieces of the puzzle still required for our ideas to work. All are rational reasons for keeping us stymied at the starting gate until we actually pull the trigger and begin.

The businessman, Napoleon Hill, who wrote *Think and Grow Rich*, once said, "The most mediocre idea acted upon is far more valuable than a flash of genius that resides only in your mind."[67] So escape the paralysis you are stuck in and act upon your idea. Let me give you three simple actions you can take immediately.

- **First, write down your goals and three action steps that will help you accomplish them**—This will automatically cause you to focus your efforts and prioritize the important steps you need to take. It is critical that you have great clarity as to where you want to go and the initial steps required. Please understand that I am not suggesting that you must understand or even outline the entire process. In fact, you will likely not know all the steps that will be required through completion of the project or achievement of the goal. But you will always have a clear and vivid picture of what the end result looks like. Put the action steps in a prominent place where you will see them frequently.

- **Second, write down a deadline for completion of each action plan and record it in your calendar**—This simple act is huge because your goal now assumes importance as part of your normal schedule and not some ancillary activity or distraction to be addressed when time permits.

- **Finally, commit to complete some portion, even if small, of your action plans each week**—It is important to note that it is initially okay to take "baby steps" in this process.

The progress you make will be incremental and start moving you toward completion. There is nothing wrong with small incremental steps. Let me illustrate this with a sports analogy. If you are a professional baseball player with a hitting average of .280 (you get a hit 28% of your times at bat), and you get just one extra hit every 36 times at bat, or just one extra hit every nine games, three things will happen to you. You will become a better than .300 hitter, you will make about $10 million more a year in compensation, and you will ultimately get inducted into the Baseball Hall of Fame.[68] Small incremental steps can be monumental in creating a bias for action.

## 2. Face your fears

Perhaps the most significant enemy we face in our pursuit of the "two in the bush" is some form of fear; fear of losing our job, fear of failure, fear of embarrassment, or fear of losing respect. All are very real obstacles and, in many instances, just plain scary! Fear is normal and many a businessman or woman has lain awake at night worrying about a budget deficit, a difficult or unhappy client, a project gone awry, a payroll to be made, or pending lawsuit. Most of the time, in normal business situations, we are able to manage our fears, in part, because we have no other choice or because we have other employees that help share the fear as a group. The situation demands a solution, and we work as a group to find one that hopefully optimizes our overall position. What happens in those situations that are not routine, e.g., when we are considering a career change, starting a new company, writing a first novel, initiating a new project, or pursuing an elusive dream? What happens when we don't have the security of corporate support or peer support and fear literally paralyzes us and keeps us from taking action or moving beyond where we are? How do we overcome the fear that prevents us from taking risks that are necessary to move beyond the status quo to pursue the extraordinary?

Dr. Linda Sapadin, in her book *Master Your Fears*, offers instructive advice around overcoming fears that keep us from moving forward with life. She talks about adaptive fear as a "nuanced emotion that diminishes during times of relative safety versus maladaptive fear that lurks beneath the surface all the time, quick to make its presence known whenever there is discomfort, the unknown or change."[69] Adaptive fear can help us avoid danger and survive, while maladaptive fear can paralyze us and undermine our ability to think clearly and make critical decisions on a timely basis. Dr. Sapadin notes several suggestions for overcoming these maladaptive fears including, among others, "thinking versus obsessing, avoiding analysis paralysis, brainstorming in the opposite direction, reframing the situation, and freeing yourself from the outcome."[70]

The concept, of course, is to take actions that force your

mind to change its attitudinal course from a negative direction to a positive one. Rather than focusing only on the extremes and negative aspects of a situation, balance your thoughts more holistically and recognize the positive aspects as well. Do your homework on the problem. Create a bias for action rather than making research and analysis the goal instead of an enabler toward the goal. List the issues that cause you the most fear and/or discomfort, and argue the other side of the discomfort equation with yourself. What makes you uncomfortable and what are the mitigating factors that might render your fear impotent? Remember our discussion in Chapter 1 around breaking the box that confines and restricts your thinking? Apply it now to your fears and reframe the situation to think three-dimensionally about solutions that may not have been obvious before now.

In summary, try to change your attitude to one of seeing your difficulties as challenges, not as problems and seeing yourself as a conqueror and not as a victim. Dr. Sapadin, says, "When fear takes precedence in your life, your lifestyle is oriented to accommodating the fears, and not overcoming them."[71] Change your attitude and become an overcomer and not an accommodator.

### 3. Embrace failure as a stepping-stone to success

In your quest to become Extraordinary, you will undoubtedly fail, perhaps numerous times. The magic is to view failure as a process rather than an event. The pages of history are littered with hundreds of examples of extraordinary people who were miserable failures: Thomas Edison who tried 1,000 materials before he made the light bulb work; Vincent van Gogh who only sold one painting in his lifetime; J.K. Rowling who, as a penniless single mom, was rejected twelve times before someone finally published *Harry Potter*; Stephen Spielberg who was denied entrance twice to University of Southern California's film school; and Colonel Sanders who, with just a $105 social security check to his name, at the age of 65, set out to sell his franchised chicken model to restaurants across the country and was rejected by 1,009 restaurants before one agreed to his idea.[72]

Failure is not the end; it is a stepping-stone to your success. Let me give you six ways to confront and master your failures.

- **Don't let failure make you a victim**—A human reaction to failure is to look for someone to blame in an attempt to assuage the frustration we feel when something did not go right. Victims feel defenseless and seek shelter from the proverbial storm they are facing. Victims can easily lose perspective and their will to fight is diminished. Don't let yourself become a victim! Take a few days if you must and wallow in your loss, but never take your eye off your goal. Tell yourself out loud, tell others about your failure, and then pick yourself up and keep moving forward. Remember, failure is just a stepping-stone to your extraordinary success.

- **Digest and learn from your failures**—Experience is not a great teacher if you never learn from it; it only makes you older. Failure, on the other hand, can be an asset if you take time to understand what went wrong and how you can prevent it from happening in the future. When you face a failure, write down the experience and consider the internal and external factors that contributed to the problems. During the American Civil War, the Federal military leaders initiated a practice they called the Staff Ride.[73] After a major battle, the generals and other leaders would literally ride the battlefield on horseback, and consider the political, operational, strategic, and tactical issues that contributed to their success or failure. These could include communications failures, supply line issues, failure of leaders to understand a superior officer's intent, missing or incomplete information about the enemy, etc. The concept of the Staff Ride is one you can implement in assessing your failures. By examining all the elements that went into your planning and execution, you can turn your failed experience into a veritable laboratory for planning your next attempt. Be deliberate and clinical in the process. You are not making excuses for yourself, but rather exploring specifics that will make your next attempt successful.

- **Don't believe that failure makes you a bad person**—It is almost impossible to separate a failure from your personal self-esteem. Remind yourself that some of the most extraordinary accomplishments in the last one hundred years came after years of repeated failure. If you fail, you are in good company; it does not make you a failure, it makes you a warrior or, if you prefer, a Jedi Knight. Don't make the mistake of blurring the lines between someone who made a mistake and someone who never does anything right. There are hundreds of quotes from famous people that I could use to inspire you. Let me try just one from arguably the best NBA basketball player of all time. Michael Jordan, a player who was rejected from his varsity high school basketball team said, "I've missed more than 9,000 shots in my career. I've lost almost 300 games. Twenty-six times I've been trusted to take the game winning shot and missed. I've failed over and over and over again in my life. And that is why I succeed."[74]

- **Build confidence by trusting your instincts**—I have made hundreds of mistakes in my life and have experienced more than a few significant failures. One thing my experience has taught me is to trust my instincts. I don't always have the discipline to follow my instincts, but I always trust my instincts. I am sure you have had an experience where you made a mistake, and in hindsight you found yourself saying, "Why did I do that? I knew better, but I just didn't do it." Or how often have you played Trivial Pursuit with a group, and, after giving a wrong answer and hearing the correct one, you said out loud, "I knew that answer, I just didn't think I did." The answer to both examples is that you instinctively knew the right answer, but you didn't trust your "gut" or your instincts.

Why is "trusting your gut" so powerful? Because your gut has been cataloging a whole lot of information for as long as you've been alive. "Trusting your gut is relying upon the collection of all your subconscious experiences," says Melody Wilding, a licensed therapist and professor of human behavior at Hunter College. As she explains, "Your gut is this collection of heuristic shortcuts. It's this unconscious-conscious learned experience center that you can draw on from your years of being alive. It holds insights that aren't immediately available to your conscious mind right now, but they're all things that you've learned and felt. In the moment, we might not be readily able to access specific information, but our gut has it at the ready."[75] When you fail, reflect back on your decision-making process. Did you trust your analysis and ignore your gut? Learn to trust your instincts. You have a reservoir of experience inside you. Learn to trust it; your gut just might be the edge you need to turn failure into success.

- **Learn to be comfortable in the "Red Zone"**—ESPN has a show during the American football season called *The Red Zone* where the broadcast switches back and forth among all games being played to allow the viewer to see every significant play occurring when a team gets inside the 20-yard line. The tension is constant for the viewing audience because every play in the Red Zone is a scoring situation where minor mistakes can be costly to one of the teams. While there is extreme tension experienced by the football fans watching this intense competition, the players never look any different. They seem calm and are able to play their normal game regardless of the stakes at hand. Do you know why? Because they practice over and over for this very situation and when they find themselves in the Red Zone, they don't have to rethink strategy or second guess their approach. They simply execute on the plan that they have practiced time and time again.

  In your quest to become Extraordinary, you will live a lot of your life in the Red Zone where emotions run high, every decision is critical, and the fear of failure palpable. During these high pressure moments, default to your principles and your core strategy. Trust your instincts and learn to be comfortable executing your game plan. Your past failures only reinforce what you have learned and provide a road map that will guide you around the obstacles that might otherwise prevent your success.

- **Be honest and deliberate in assessing failures**—Failure can be an asset if you allow it to be your guide in navigating the future. In doing so, you have to be brutally honest and almost clinical in analyzing your past mistakes. This bias-free analysis is essential because it is so difficult to self-diagnose our failures and so easy to be beguiled into believing that they are either not our fault, or that they are not as bad as they seem. Lay out your past failures front and center and face them head-on. Analyze the reasons they occurred and what they have taught you for the future. Build the failure findings into your new plan, and then walk away from them. Your failures are no longer obstacles that weigh you down, but are stepping-stones to your future success.

## 4. Find role models for courage and learn from them

It takes courage to fail multiple times and then keep coming back to try again and again. But as we have already demonstrated, there are hundreds of stories of ordinary people who accomplished extraordinary things because they would never quit or take no for an answer. Let these courageous people motivate you to try and try again, whether it's Stephen King whose first novel was rejected thirty-seven times, or the multiple numbers of current day heroes and legends like Walt Disney and Oprah Winfrey who were fired from early jobs and told they lacked what it would take to be successful in their chosen professions.[76] Let them inspire you to never take no for an answer, to never accept the status quo, and to keep trying in the face of seemingly unsurmountable obstacles. But don't stop with heroes and legends; look around the corner of your cubicle or down the street in your neighborhood and find those ordinary people—often from among your own friends—who are indefatigable at what they do. Find people who always have a positive attitude, who take responsibility for their failures. Learn from them and in the words of the great British Prime Minister Winston Churchill, "never, never, never give up."[77]

## 5. Know your limitations and never risk it all

In your quest to become Extraordinary, it is important to remember that there is a tremendous difference between taking risks and gambling. The gambler is cavalier, rolls the dice, and doesn't hesitate to "let it all ride on Red 23." Consider this quote from *33 Strategies of War* by Robert Greene: "The great German general Erwin Rommel once made a distinction between a gamble and a risk. Both cases involve an action with only a chance of success, a chance that is heightened by acting with boldness. The difference is that with risk, if you lose, you can recover: your reputation will suffer no long-term damage, your resources will not be depleted, and you can return to your original position with acceptable losses. With a gamble, on the other hand, defeat can lead to a slew of problems that are likely to spiral out of control. If you encounter difficulties in a gamble, it becomes harder to pull out—you realize that the stakes are too high; you cannot afford to lose. So you try harder to rescue the situation, often making it worse and sinking deeper into the hole that you cannot get out of...Taking risks is essential; gambling is foolhardy." [78]

Rommel's advice is worth noting, as is the line uttered by Clint Eastwood in his role in the movie *Magnum Force*. Eastwood's character, Harry Callahan, famously reminded us that "a man's got to know his limitations."[79] In other words, be a risk-taker, but not a gambler. Many years ago, I had a client who kept a poster on his wall as a reminder of this risk-taker/gambler admonition. The poster depicted a stock table from the *Wall Street Journal* the day after Monday, October 19, 1987, (referred to as Black Monday) when the market crashed, losing huge value in a very short time. The Dow Jones Industrial Average (DJIA) fell exactly 508 points on that day. Across the stock chart were the emblazoned words, "Risk Not Thy Whole Wad."[80]

Enough said!

## The Journey to Extraordinary:
## Tips for the Traveler...

Extraordinary people are not shackled by the need to protect what they have, but continuously inspired by the vision of how much more the future can bring. They are not willing to settle for what is "in hand," whether it is a mediocre job, a good performance report, a tried and true process, or the next satisfactory outcome. They see an exploding career that exceeds expectations, innovation that renders tried and true as tired and timid, and ever-improving results that make satisfactory outcomes seem as old and quaint as dial-up internet. In short, extraordinary people are never satisfied with a "bird in the hand." And therein lies the problem.

Lead the effort to prove that the old idiom should be revised to read, "A bird in the hand of the 'average' man or woman is worth two in the bush."

# CHAPTER 7

## Haste Makes Waste

### Accelerate the Pace; Time Is Not Your Friend

This mythical warning appears to have been first recorded in 1575 as "Stop trying to rush through things at once— haste makes waste, you know."[81] It was later recorded in John Ray's 1678 proverb collection as a rhyming text, "Haste makes waste, and waste makes want, and want makes strife between the good man and his wife."[82] No matter the source, the idea is clear. If you hurry through a project or activity, you will ultimately waste more time than you hoped to save by your speedy process. This anecdotal advice has often been given by parents to their children, by teachers to their students, and in a whole variety of workplace environments where employers were trying to ensure a quality product. The problem, however, is that the old idiom is just not true and earns a prominent position in my growing list of mythical sayings that breed mediocrity.

The fundamental issue is that the assumption, albeit false, is that speed and quality cannot coexist together; you can have speed or quality, but you cannot have both at the same time. We have all heard this same opinion repeated in the corporate environment phrased as "Good, cheap, fast—pick two." If you select good and fast, then it will not be cheap. If you select good and cheap, then it won't be completed very fast. And if you pick cheap and fast, the quality will not be good. This idea pits quality and speedy decision-making against each other in an intellectual battle that has no possible winner unless you have no budget constraints, or you are willing to pay extravagantly to link quality and speed.

A hundred years ago, it might have made sense to simply drop the argument and stipulate that skilled work like carpentry, craftsmanship, or architecture required a minimum level of time to complete, and hence it was literally impossible to deliver excellence at a reasonable price. Fortunately, manufacturing technologies, supply-chain linkage, process improvement, and quality control systems have all but rendered the old "haste makes waste" idiom obsolete. And if you think the application is only relevant to the crafts or manufacturing industries, consider the service industries like the accounting profession where the work of a tax accountant in years as late as the 1970s can now be performed on mobile devices like a smartphone. Clearly, speed has not only made a lasting imprint on the efficiency of today's workforce, but has also contributed mightily—in a cause and effect relationship—to the quality of work product.

The more insidious consequence, however, of the "haste makes waste" jargon in today's environment is its application to the broader circle of general decision-making. The overwhelming amount of data that technology now makes possible, and the seemingly unlimited access to fact, fiction, and opinion residing on the internet or cloud, has created an unintended consequence where anyone who is engaged, personally or professionally, in decision-making is at best impeded by the sheer volume of input, data points, and other information to be considered, and at worst rendered indecisive by the burden of so many choices. This dilemma is not limited just to the young family buying a new automobile, but to middle managers in the bowels of corporate America, to executives in the C-Suites of Fortune 1000 companies, and to aspiring professionals and businesspeople like you who are considering a new career, planning an entrepreneurial start-up, or pursuing a passion that has intermittently flamed and flickered for years. The decisions being made by all of these groups require enough information to make an informed judgment, but time is not usually on their side. Deadlines may not be met, interest rates may go up, competitive bids may be lost, regulations may change, employees may resign, competitive advantage may be lost, or red hot opportunities that feed a passion might flicker and extinguish forever.

If you believe what the majority of executive coaches in the United States believe, indecision in both public and private companies is ubiquitous. Even when CEOs are decisive, the culture of many organizations is to render the decision ineffective through a series of corporate or regional strategy, marketing, and operational inactions by managers who are more concerned with individual performance than overall corporate performance. In these situations, delay and procrastination undermine the mission of the business and ultimately cost the shareholders of the company. These are cases where a little hasty decision-making would not have created "waste," but very well may have saved the Company and its shareholders a lot of money.

Indecision or slowness in making decisions in any organization, or in your personal life, is generally not caused by a lack of information. It is not related to or affected by what we already know. Rather, it is the fear of the unknown or what we don't know—the unknown unknowns or Unk Unks, as they have been colloquially christened in the engineering world, that paralyze us into inaction. We have done the research, we have sought the advice of consultants, we have talked with subject-matter experts, but we still worry about the Unk Unks. We wring hands and metaphorically jump hoops and worry ourselves into indecision over the unknown. No one would ever accuse us of making a hasty decision. In fact, they would assume that, in light of our thorough and lengthy process, we absolutely subscribed to the old saying that "haste makes waste." But what if I told you that there was compelling evidence to suggest that the solution to this dilemma is not more research or more time, but rather less time and a quicker decision process? What if I told you that frequently haste does not make waste, but actually quite the opposite—it produces better results?

Psychologists and scientists in recent years have been debating vigorously the question of whether intuitive thinking versus analytical thinking is more effective in making decisions where there is a great deal of uncertainty. In his 2014 article in the *Harvard Business Review,* "Instinct Can Beat Analytical Thinking," Justin Fox writes, "Researchers have confronted us in recent years with example after example of how we humans get things wrong when it comes to making decisions. We misunderstand probability, we're myopic, we pay attention to the wrong things, and we just generally mess up. This popular triumph of the "heuristics and biases" literature pioneered by psychologists Daniel Kahneman and Amos Tversky has made us aware of flaws that economists long glossed over, and led to interesting innovations in retirement planning and government policy. It is not, however, the only lens through which to view decision-making."[83]

Psychologist Gerd Gigerenzer has spent his career focusing on the ways in which we get things *right*, or could at least learn to. In Gigerenzer's view, using heuristics, rules of thumb, and other shortcuts often lead to better decisions than the models of "rational" decision-making developed by mathematicians and statisticians. Dr. Gigerenzer says it this way: "Gut feelings are tools for an uncertain world. They're not caprice. They are not a sixth sense or God's voice. They are based on lots of experience, an unconscious form of intelligence. I've worked with large companies and asked decision-makers how often they base an important professional decision on that gut feeling. In the companies I've worked with, which are large international companies, about half of all decisions are, at the end, a gut decision. But the same managers would never admit this in public. There's fear of being made responsible if something goes wrong, so they have developed a few strategies to deal with this fear. One is to find reasons after the fact. A top manager may have a gut feeling, but then he asks an employee to find facts in the next two weeks, and thereafter the decision is presented as a fact-based, big-data-based decision. That's a waste of time, intelligence, and money. The more expensive version is to hire a consulting company, which will provide a 200-page document to justify the gut feeling. And then there is the most expensive version, namely defensive decision-making. Here, a manager feels he should go with option A, but if something goes wrong, he can't explain it, so that's not good. So he recommends option B, something of a secondary or third-class choice. Defensive decision-making hurts the company and protects the decision-maker. In the consulting projects I've done with large companies, it happens in about a third to half of all important project-related decisions. You can imagine how much these companies lose."[84]

In his book, *Blink: the Power of Thinking Without Thinking*, Malcolm Gladwell says, "This new notion of the adaptive unconscious is thought of as a kind of giant computer that quickly and quietly processes a lot of the data we need in order to keep functioning as human beings…I think we are innately suspicious of this kind of rapid cognition. We live in a world that assumes that the quality of a decision is directly related to the time and effort that went into making it. When doctors are faced with a difficult diagnosis, they order more tests, and when we are uncertain about what we hear, we ask for a second opinion. And what do we tell our children? Haste makes waste. Look before you leap. Stop and think. Don't judge a book by its cover. We believe that we are always better off gathering as much information as possible and spending as much time as possible in deliberation. We really don't trust conscious decision-making. But there are moments, particularly in times of stress, when haste does not make waste, when our snap judgments and first impressions can offer a much better means of making sense of the world."[85] And finally, Timothy Wilson writes in his book *Strangers to Ourselves*: "The mind operates most efficiently by relegating a good deal of high-level, sophisticated thinking to the unconscious, just as a modern jetliner is able to fly on automatic pilot with little or no input from the human, 'conscious' pilot. The adaptive unconscious does an excellent job of sizing up the world, warning people of danger, setting goals, and initiating action in a sophisticated and efficient manner."[85]

Clearly, there are times when there is no substitute for deep analytical thinking and more information and more time is required. Hopefully, however, the aforementioned scholarly research, which is only a sheer abstract of the substantive work done on the subject, is persuasive. There are times, more often than we are willing to admit, when our instincts are better, when we do not need more time or information, and when haste does, indeed, not make waste. There are times when we truly should just "trust our gut."

Regardless of where you stand on the debate between intuitive versus analytical thinking, let me give you five things you can do to improve the speed of your decision-making. And I would argue that it will affect the quality and effectiveness of your decision-making as well.

• **Use the Rule of Three to help prioritize the critical and most relevant issues related to your decision and to dampen the noise around the process**—In the process of researching the issues that must be understood to make a good decision, we gather a lot of information and data points that are interesting, but ultimately are not important to the decision at hand. In fact, we often gather substantially more information than we actually need. Over the decision-making process, most of this data is filtered out as useless or nonrelevant, but invariably there are tangential issues that stay around the fringes and are just relevant enough to keep us from disposing of them too quickly. Often, these bits of information are necessary for the ultimate execution of the decision, but not actually required for us to make the decision. This is especially true if there is uncertainty in several of the facts we are considering, if there is a large number of constituencies affected by the decision, or if there are different positive or adverse reactions that could result from the decision.

When you are trying to satisfy numerous objectives for numerous stakeholders, you are doomed from the beginning. You have to decide the most important objectives and those that are absolutely critical to your problem-solving mission. I have discovered that an effective way to manage and accelerate the decision process is to articulate the problem into no more than three big issues. This literally forces me to ignore the lesser issues while I devote my attention to the big issues that must be solved. I first learned this technique many years ago from my mentor, Ed Harris, the then managing partner of the Atlanta office of Price Waterhouse. No matter the nature of the problem or issue being considered, Ed had the uncanny ability to see through the haze created by sometimes hundreds of facts and circumstances and single out the two or three critical issues that really mattered in reaching a decision. I originally attributed this to Ed's superior intellect, but over time I realized that he was teaching me a valuable lesson in focus and prioritization—a lesson that I could learn. And you can learn it too; it just takes practice.

- **Avoid information creep**—In spite of your efforts to prioritize the issues surrounding your decision-making process, there will always be a tendency to let other facts or data points influence your thinking. The constant vigilance for information that might affect your decision, or result in a better decision, is not only necessary but is entirely appropriate. To do otherwise would be akin to "putting your head in the sand."

Notwithstanding the benefits of constant diligence, it is easy to be beguiled by the ubiquitous information that is literally at your fingertips. Learn to quickly distinguish between interesting data and data that is actually relevant to the decision at hand and dispose of the irrelevant. All too often, decision-makers fall into the trap of keeping a little of both.

One of my early mentors explained it to me in language that I have never forgotten. He explained it this way.

Suppose you have one handful of horse manure and the other full of rose petals. You look at the one hand; it looks like rose petals, feels like rose petals, and smells like rose petals. Then you look at the other hand. It feels like manure, it looks like manure, and it smells like manure. So what do you do? Unfortunately, as my mentor described, many decision-makers are loath to dispose of any information they have, and so they put both hands in their pockets. Warning! The decision process bogs down when good information is blended with irrelevant information. Clarity is obscured, and the process gets messy.

- **Use the old 80/20 rule for determining when you have gathered enough data and information**—Rita McGrath, a professor at Columbia University and an expert in building competitive advantage through transient strategies says that, in the future, "fast and roughly right decision-making will replace deliberations that are precise but slow. Speed is paramount."[87] Increasing the speed of decision-making can be problematic, however, in environments where there is a seemingly endless supply of data that must be read, understood, and interpreted. How do you determine when you have enough information to make the right decision? And even if you could gather all the available information, how would you efficiently process it? One way to increase the speed of your decision-making and to reduce the level of your frustration is to acknowledge the old Pareto's Law that posits that 20% of the invested input is responsible for 80% of the results obtained.[88] There is a point at beyond which more data will not improve the efficacy of your decision. While we often use Pareto's Law anecdotally, there is scientific research to support the view that more information is not better, and that there may be a point at which we can reach a satisfactory decision without additional input.

Dr. Herbert Simon was an American economist who developed a theory about economic decision-making that he called "satisficing," a combination of the words "satisfy" and "suffice."[89] In a 2009 profile of Dr. Simon, *The Economist* magazine noted that "Contrary to the tenets of classical economics, Simon maintained that individuals do not seek to maximize their benefit from a particular course of action (since they cannot assimilate and digest all the information that would be needed to do such a thing). Not only can they not get access to all the information required, but even if they could, their minds would be unable to process it properly." The human mind necessarily restricts itself. It is, as Simon put it, bounded by "cognitive limits."[90] Hence people, in many different situations, seek something that is "good enough," something that is satisfactory. This real-world behavior is what Simon called "satisficing." Before you spend hours parsing data that may not be relevant or useful, take a step back and ask, "What critical information am I missing that I must have in order to make a decision?" It might be that you have already reached a "roughly right" or "satisficing" decision.

- **Seek another opinion before deciding**—Psychologists have long argued that one of the big issues around decision-making is the cognitive bias that is built into us from our education, our past experiences, and our upbringing. These biases present two problems. First, they may prevent us from reaching the right decision because we can only see our biased perspective, and second, we may wrestle or debate with ourselves too long over difficult issues without realizing that our knowledge and intellect are in conflict with those biases.

  Most people appreciate, if only anecdotally, the value in seeking others opinions, and we do it informally all the time. Nick Tasler, the CEO of Decision Pulse believes that consulting others will speed up the decision process. In his *Harvard Business Review* article, "Make Good Decisions Faster," Tasler talks about consulting one or two key "anti-yous" to get a perspective outside yourself. Tasler says, "Consulting an anti-you works in two ways. The act of explaining your situation to another person often gives you new insights about the decision before the other person even responds. And the fresh perspective they offer in response is the second bonus."[91] In other words, the sheer act of sharing a problem with a colleague has a positive benefit because you are required to articulate the issue or problem to someone who does not understand it as well as you.

In teaching advanced accounting to graduate-level college students, a subject in which I am an expert, I find that articulating the subject matter to students who have little knowledge and asking them fundamental questions actually deepens my knowledge of the material. Similarly, sharing issues related to decisions with colleagues can open your mind to a perspective that you simply did not have. The real magic happens when you are able to share issues or problems with Tasler's "anti-you" who does not think like you and is likely to pushback or challenge your current thinking.

• **Set a definitive deadline for making a decision**—How often have you been in a meeting where there was unanimous agreement on how a decision process was to move forward and everyone left feeling really good about the process? But then several weeks pass and nothing happens. Sound familiar? Of course it does; it happens every day in corporate America and in nonprofit organizations across the country. Businessmen and women fall prey to a variety of committed sins that keep them from taking decisive action. They all have good intentions when they leave the meeting, but as my grandmother used to caution me, "The road to Hell is paved with good intentions." Major among these sins is procrastination, the intentional act of putting off or delaying something that requires immediate attention. It is important to note that this definition does not include "forgetting, overlooking, or misunderstanding." Rather, it is the proactive, intentional act of putting off a task.

Procrastination, in some form or another, is often at the heart of a delayed or slow decision process. While I call it an intentional sin, it is not necessarily malicious, but almost always insidious. It starts with a well-meaning delay to work on other pressing matters of business or commerce and slowly, but surely, the matter at hand gets pushed further and further back in the decision queue. The more days pass without action, the easier it is to shuffle the matter to a lower priority because other matters now look more important. Imagine an entire organization with its many component parts operating on this basis. It does not take long to realize why there have been so many books written around making faster and more effective decisions.

Let me give you a simple and direct way to stop living in sin. Whether you are in a meeting as a leader or as a participant, never, ever leave the meeting without everyone having a definitive action item to complete and a date by which it must be completed. The date needs to be specific and calendared by everyone. The formality of the process is important because it automatically elevates the priority and portends a penalty, real or imagined, if the date is not met. The purpose, of course, is focus, and it takes a deadline to focus most busy people. Deadlines for making decisions not only provide individual focus; they also help ensure 1) a shared responsibility among team members, 2) a common goal that is published and well known, and 3) a sense of urgency that demands action. These three in concert will help speed your decision-making process and, hopefully, improve the outcome.

Remember, in your pursuit of the extraordinary, time is not your friend and haste does not make waste. Other professionals are competing for your clients, competitors are targeting your customers, and aggressive managers are looking for your job. You must be a transient decision-maker who goes overboard in preparation, but then does not hesitate to pull the trigger and decide. Mark Feldman and Michael Spratt, in their book *Five Frogs on a Log: A CEO's Field Guide to Accelerating the Transition in Mergers, Acquisitions, and Gut Wrenching Change*, remind us of an old riddle that said:

> "Five frogs sat on a log,
> Four of them decided to jump off,
> How many frogs are left on the log?"[92]

Think about it a minute before you answer. The answer: all five frogs are left. Why? Because there is a big difference in deciding to jump and jumping. Average depends on indecision; Extraordinary requires a "Jumper."

## The Journey to Extraordinary:
## Tips for the Traveler...

Time is not your friend when making decisions. Avoid information creep, never procrastinate and eliminate data that is interesting, but irrelevant to your decision process. Remember the warning of the rose petals and the manure! The decision process bogs down when good information is blended with irrelevant data; clarity is obscured, and the process gets messy.

# CHAPTER 8

# Don't Bite Off More Than You Can Chew

## Demand Hard Work

The origin of this old saying may be unclear, but its meaning is not—it transcends generations from the early 1900s, through the Baby Boomers and Generation Xer's, and to the Millennials of today. Most historical sources suggest that originally the phrase referred to "taking a bite" off a plug (or block) of chewing tobacco, and the admonition was to be careful not to bite off more of the potent material than your mouth could handle at one time. While the literal meaning might still be relevant, it is the metaphorical meaning that has created an enduring place in our idiomatic communications with each other. "Don't bite off more than you can chew" means don't take on more than you can handle, don't take on excessive responsibility, don't overdo it, and numerous other cautionary warnings about the perils of trying to do too much at one time.

I include this "old rule" in my top ten list of cultural mandates that need to be revisited and refined because I believe it has become a quiet mantra for Average, an anecdotal acceptance that "just enough" is okay, that "meets expectations" is satisfactory performance, and that the willingness to work hard and take on inordinate responsibility is to be eschewed in favor of the status quo. This book is about redefining rules that have constrained us personally and professionally. It's about a quest to overcome Average and become Exceptional. It's about taking on more than you can chew and realizing the accomplishment and fulfillment that comes from just plain old hard work.

"Don't bite off more than you can chew" may sound benign or even helpful for people who tend to overcommit and then fail to keep their promises, but there is an invisible premise inherent in the saying that has become amplified over the last twenty years in American culture. That premise is that individual effort and exceptionalism is not as important as acceptance and self-esteem. In the interest of inclusion and fairness, parents and educators have promoted an environment of entitlement where everyone gets assigned to a team and every team member gets a trophy for their individual efforts. While the intent has been admirable, the result has been to create a homogeneous population where Average is rewarded just the same as Exceptional. Students who should have been held back in a grade are given promotions to avoid both the stigma to parent and child, and to protect the reputation of the teacher who has children who are failing. Rather than teaching this future workforce the value of hard work and the lessons of failure, the attention is focused on creating self-esteem and perpetuating the myth that moving in lock-step as Average is acceptable.

If you think I am being harsh in my judgment, listen to Eric Chester, author of the book, *Reviving Work Ethic*. In discussing his children and, more broadly, the population between the ages of twenty-six and thirty-one, Chester says, "They've grown up in a world where most people work hard to find ways of avoiding hard work. They've heard stories telling how lottery winners, day traders, bloggers, dot-commers, and internet marketers have managed to beat the system and derive a huge bounty with little or no effort. They've been inundated with reality television that turns talentless fools into millionaires in the blink of an eye and with the greatest of ease. To them, an apprentice is not a young worker learning a trade at the foot of a master craftsman, but rather a devious schemer finagling to get a co-worker fired by Donald Trump. Not surprisingly, *The 4-Hour Workweek* is more than a national bestselling book; it's a rallying cry."[93]

The American work ethic has been debated by politicians and businesspeople alike over the last several years with intense focus on comparing and contrasting the Baby Boomers (1946-1964) and Gen Xers (1965-1980) with the Gen Ys/ Millennials (1980-present). Politicians are concerned primarily with voting trends and determining how the burgeoning Millennial population can be attracted to their particular political parties, while the business community is faced with enormous cultural changes as Baby Boomers continue retiring, Gen Xers settle in for the last third of their work lives and Millennials become the dominate force in the workplace. Business leaders are asking, "How do we attract and retain this new pool of talent and what makes them tick?" The Pew Research Center did an exhaustive study on Millennials in 2010 focusing on a variety of issues including, among others, political leanings, technology, social issues, work and play, and religion. The following chart from the Pew Report summarizes the top five answers of the respective population groups to a single, open-ended question, "What makes your generation unique?"[94]

The chart is interesting in its stark contrast among the four population groups as to their views on work ethic. It is not surprising to see the dominate position of work ethic with the Boomers. We have known for a while that this group, often the first in the family to go to college, was motivated to work and "do better" than their parents. After a short foray into social protest in the 1960s, they settled into a work environment where personal and work lives blended and became almost indistinguishable. Work dominated their lives and it was this group that we first began calling "workaholics." The Gen Xers are not far behind the Millennials in defining themselves with work ethic, especially when you add in technology, which most of them would likely suggest is synonymous or part and parcel with their work. This generation was the first to embrace technology (computers, screens in various formats, and the internet) from their youth to adulthood, and technology was more than just a tool. It became a way of life at work and at home.

## What Makes Your Generation Unique?

### Millennial
1. Technology use (24%)
2. Music/Pop culture (11%)
3. Liberal/tolerant (7%)
4. Smarter (6%)
5. Clothes (5%)

### Boomer
1. Work ethic (17%)
2. Respectful (14%)
3. Values/Morals (8%)
4. "Baby Boomers" (6%)
5. Smarter (5%)

### Gen X
1. Technology use (12%)
2. Work ethic (11%)
3. Conservative/Trad'l (7%)
4. Smarter (5%)
5. Respectful (5%)

### Silent
1. WWII, Depression (14%)
2. Smarter (13%)
3. Honest (12%)
4. Work ethic (10%)
5. Values/Morals (10%)

Note: Based on respondents who said their generation was unique/distinct. Items represent individual, open-ended responses. Top five responses are shown for each age group. Sample sizes for sub-groups are as follows: Millennials, n=527; Gen X, n=173; Boomers, n=283; Silent, n=205.

And then there are the Millennials. Unlike the other four groups, work ethic does not make their top five defining characteristics. They define themselves by their technology and their music. The Pew Research Center notes that technology is universal amongst this group. The Center noted that "Millennials' technological exceptionalism is chronicled throughout the survey. It's not just their gadgets—it's the way they've fused their social lives into them. For example, three-quarters of Millennials have created a profile on a social networking site, compared with half of Gen Xers, 30% of the Boomers, and 6% of Silents." The Survey explores the Millennials' attitude toward work and employment and the research suggests that this young population group is by no means lazy or afraid of work; they just view it differently.[95]

Take for example, my case of Bob and Paul (not their real names), two brothers who, with their father, run and own a thriving family business in the lower middle market. Bob, the older brother, is a young Gen Xer while the younger Paul is a mid-level Millennial. Both brothers are college-educated, although Paul has an advanced graduate degree, and both had business careers before joining their father in the family business. In developing a strategic plan for the business, I spent substantial time with both brothers and their father, individually and as a group, discussing their respective roles in the company, their views of each other, their individual work ethic, and their perspectives on how the company and its employees could work more collaboratively. The results of this process were fascinating and provided a glimpse into the generational and cultural divide that exists between Boomers, Gen Xers, and Millennials, especially with respect to work ethic. First, both brothers had deep and genuine respect for their father, an early, first-level Boomer. They acknowledged that he worked substantially harder than they did and they were appreciative of his hard work. Dad agreed with his sons and believed that neither of them worked hard because they felt "entitled." Simultaneously, Bob and Paul were dismissive of their father's interest in every detail of the business and believed that it was time for him to retire and let the younger generation take over completely. The brothers were generally in lockstep with this belief and with most issues dealing with Dad, but their similarities stopped there. The following summarizes their differing perspectives.

| Bob, *Gen X* | Paul, *Millennial* |
| --- | --- |
| Paul is lazy and doesn't work enough. | I work smart; I don't need 12 hours a day. |
| Paul lives in another city and is not engaged. | Location doesn't matter; we have Facetime. |
| Paul lacks a sense of urgency. | Bob operates in panic mode and is disruptive. |
| Paul is usually late and misses meetings. | Administrative meetings are a waste of time. |
| Paul always puts his personal life over work. | Who cares as long as I get my work done? |

Both Bob and Paul will tell you that they believe in hard work, but they are not willing to work as hard as Dad did, nor should anyone expect them to. They believe that their personal time is just as important as their work life, but they see work and personal time as distinctly separate modules of their life that can be bifurcated and not combined. Dad blames himself for this seismic shift between his and their generations. He paid for their school, "gave" them the Company, and they never learned the value of hard work in achieving what they now have.

So, is this just a generational issue that reflects the changing social values between the younger workforce and their older counterparts, driven in part by technology? Similar to Boomers who cut their long hair, found their discarded bras, and donned pinstripe suits and high heels as they exited the 1970s, will the Millennials' change their seemingly lackadaisical attitudes toward work as they get older? Is it just a matter of differing perspectives like those of Bob and Paul and, in effect, do we need to redefine "work ethic" to take into consideration the new technologies and social structure of a modern economy? Or, has there really been a serious diminution in the American work ethic and the values it represents?

Eric Chester would answer with a resounding yes to this last question. In *Reviving Work Ethic*, Chester says, "Work has degenerated to little more than a four letter word; a necessary evil. It's no longer viewed as something to be proud of, but rather something to disdain, to shortcut, or to elude all together."[96] In other words, our future workforce in America has succumbed to the treacherous belief that Average is okay, that a limited work week is preferable, and that hard work is way overstated. Discouraging to say the least; but I believe there is hope.

While writing this book, I was returning from a trip to South Florida and on the train from a remote terminal to baggage claim, I noticed a young man standing next to me in work clothes, most likely an outside baggage worker. He was intently reading a large notebook and periodically making notes and changes. I was intrigued so I asked if he was a student and if he was doing homework. He looked up and said, "No, I'm a songwriter and I'm just getting off work." He acknowledged that he had not yet sold any of what appeared to be fifty pages of songs in the book, but said, "If I keep working hard at it, I'll make it." He walked away still reading and writing, and I followed him up the escalator inspired by both his dream and his work ethic. He had a full-time job, but he was biting off more than he could chew, and he was chewing it quite well.

Fascinated by this chance encounter and the findings of the Pew Research Group, I decided to do my own research with two separate groups of Millennials consisting of my day-class and evening-class graduate students. Similar to the Pew analysis, I asked the students to send me a written note with five words that describe Millennials as viewed through themselves. The following is an unedited summary of words they used:

- **Social**, young, focused, fun, self-aware
- Efficient, **progressive**, passionate, mobile, **tech-savvy**
- **Entitled, independent, opinionated, impatient**, wayfaring
- Selfish, ambitious, non-committal, travelers, dreamers
- **Entitled, multi-taskers**, diverse, impressionable, lucky
- **Connected**, immediate, travel, **technology, social**
- **Impatient, entitled, innovative, opinionated**, distracted
- Arrogant, dependent, intelligent, **social, technological**
- **Independent**, respectful, free-spirited, pressured
- **Impatient, entitled**, determined, **multi-tasker, innovative**
- Driven, passionate, curious, conscientious, active
- **Innovative**, sensitive, stubborn, enthusiastic, leaders
- **Connected, technology, progressive, impatient**, material
- **Technology, innovative, impatient**, dreamer, anti-social
- **Innovative**, believer, optimistic, educated, **impatient**
- Hard-working, work-martyr, work/life balance, **progressive**
- Educated, open-minded, kind, thoughtful, inheritors of 21st century
- Logic, life/work balance, internet, challenge, quick
- **Connected**, cultured, **impatient, independent**, empowered
- **Technology, entitlement**, informed, diverse, blessed
- Smart, detail, hard-working, patient, ambitious

✧

Words that appeared more than twice are noted in bold print. While clearly not scientific, and anecdotal at best, the experiment shed additional light on the way Millennials think. The group, without consultation with each other, concluded that they are entitled, impatient, technologically savvy, progressive, social, independent, connected and innovative. They clearly view life through more than a work lens, and are more concerned with their quality of life (free-spirited, travelers, wayfaring, dreamers, fun, and self-aware) more than their careers. They view themselves as connected socially, smart, and driven, but not to the exclusion of everything else. Interestingly enough, these are graduate students, many who already work a full day before going to class and are aspiring to a graduate degree in accounting and a new or better job at an accounting firm or in the industry.

The message should be clear to leaders who are expecting to mold these young students into hard working professionals. Managing them is radically different than it was with the Gen Xers. The Millennials are smart and want to succeed, but they may not be willing to commit the level of effort that you are expecting. The challenge is to help them achieve their non-financial objectives while working as your employee—a daunting challenge to say the least.

The real question for business leaders is how do we reignite our employees' passion for hard work? How do we teach an "entitlement" generation the value of "sweat equity"? For

Gen Xers and Millennials, the question is slightly different. In a quest for exceptionalism, how do you stand out in a crowd and look different? In light of the fact that you are all smart, you are all well educated, and you all have an Intel chip in your computer, how will you ever differentiate yourself amongst the millions of young people who want the same job you want, or worse, want the job you have? You have no intellectual advantage, no educational advantage, and certainly no advantage in technology. So, it's your move. What do you do?

Let's take these questions one at a time and map a strategy for abandoning Average and "biting off more than we can chew."

## What can leaders do to inspire hard work?

I would suggest three important steps:

**Step 1. Make the work meaningful**—The most important step that business leaders can take to inspire their people to work hard is to make the work they do meaningful. When you view the words that Millennials use to describe themselves you begin to understand that work for work's sake is not inspiring no matter how much money they are being paid. Unlike my first day as a staff accountant at Price Waterhouse, when I spent six hours moving furniture, today's new employees want to know not only why they are doing a task, but also why it matters on a grander scale. They want to understand the mission of the business, how their job fits in, and how they contribute to that overall mission. No one wants to work excessive hours when they have no clue why such hours are so critical. Conversely, when employees have a sense of the company's mission and how they are critical to its accomplishment, hard work and overtime become secondary to their focused efforts.

Perhaps the best example of this was the Apollo moon landing in 1968. For months prior to the mission, NASA employees were working literally around the clock, under extreme stress, away from their families, with no sleep and no time off. According to NASA officials, in spite of the pressure and extreme work conditions, morale at the Agency was through the roof—had never been better. Then the moon launch was successful, the celebration period began, and working hours went back to normal. Six weeks later, morale was in the pits even for those employees who were not in fear of losing their jobs. Why? Simply stated, the sense of mission had been fulfilled. The deadline that bonded them together as a team was lifted. The work became more routine and did not have as much meaning for the employees as before the launch.[97]

Meaningful work gives purpose to the hours. The best way to ensure that it happens is for leaders to continually communicate with their people about where the company is going, how it will get there, and the role they play as individuals. The mission can change, and, as it does, it is even more critical that leaders communicate. We are not all going to the moon, but companies can have a mission just as noble as NASA. Take Google, for example, which regularly communicates to their employees their mission "to organize the world's information and make it universally accessible and useful." It is not surprising that according to PayScale, a firm specializing in employee data analytics, 73% of Google employees find their jobs to be meaningful.[98] Lest you think only a company the size of Google can create meaningful work, consider Southeast Restoration, a small company in Georgia in the remodeling and remediation business whose mission is "Restoring Lives and Repairing Property." The Company's monthly newsletter, "Restored," profiles the families whose homes have been rebuilt, as well as the families of the Southeast team members. The result: a meaningful work environment where every employee from the receptionist to the CEO lives and talks the mission.[99]

Another way to create a sense of meaningful work in your company is to engage your employees in making an impact in their community. Rather than just write a check to a charity, find a way to engage your employees in the community where they can see and feel the impact that "their" company is having. When it comes to engaging employees in philanthropy and social causes, PwC, the large accounting firm, serves as a role model for other companies. PwC's "Dollars for Doers" program gives $2,500 grants to causes about which employees are passionate and work toward. Through its PwC Charitable Foundation, the company invested $47.2 million in local communities from 2001 to 2015. And, in-line with its area of expertise, PwC's U.S. practice dedicates over 150,000 pro bono hours annually to a financial literacy program called "Earn Your Future."[100] These programs cause employees to feel good about their efforts in the community and it makes them proud of the company they work for. No wonder that PwC is consistently listed in the top 100 places to work and was number 23 in 2016.

**Step 2. Make your company a fun place to work**—If you are a business leader and you want your employees to work harder at their jobs and take on more and more responsibility, you have to make work fun. I mentor numerous early-career professionals and businessmen and women, and I start our first session with the same mantra. I tell them that they should stick with their career and their existing employer as long as they can answer "yes" to three questions. First, "Am I learning something new every week?" Second, "Am I improving my marketability to other employers?" And, finally, "Am I happy and having fun?" The first two questions are obvious—you owe it to yourself, and your employer owes it to you, to ensure that you are in a learning environment where your skill set is improving. The third question is equally obvious, but much more important than the first two. I tell my mentees that the

Declaration of Independence guaranteed them three things—Life, Liberty, and the Pursuit of Happiness. Anything short of that should be a nonstarter no matter who the employer is.

Business leaders have a responsibility to ensure that their workplace is a fun environment. If you believe differently, I will refer you to the list of Pew Research words noted in their 2010 study of Millennials or the words in my anecdotal study conducted in 2017 with university graduate students, e.g., music, social, fun, connected, free-spirited, traveler, and dreamer. The Millennial generation of workers and those following them want to experience life *at work* differently than their parents. The Boomers, and even the Gen Xers, to some extent, have been married to their jobs and their personal life has often been relatively controlled and at the whim of their work schedule. The Millennials spent their childhoods observing this phenomenon, and, as they reached the workforce, they resoundingly rejected it. While they may be appropriately tagged with the rap of feeling entitled or being obsessed with themselves, they clearly do not want to work at a job or in an environment that controls their lives the way they watched work control the lives of their parents. So, as business leaders, how do we redefine work to eliminate the addiction and workaholic mentality, while simultaneously, inspiring our young employees to work harder and take on more responsibility? Let me suggest a few simple ideas that business leaders can implement, regardless of the size of their companies, that will have a disproportionate impact on how employees perceive their work environment.

- **Make flexible scheduling work for you**—Many employers have implemented some form of flexible scheduling and have recognized it as an inexpensive perk that has disproportionate benefits to its cost. The benefits include happier employees, better teaming, a demonstrable focus on family, and greater productivity. The key for employers, especially smaller, middle market companies, is to begin small and find a plan that works for your company and your people. Years ago at PwC, before flexible scheduling became fashionable, I started with a simple plan that worked for me. As a partner of the firm, I often arrived at the office late after an early morning breakfast and worked until 7 p.m. at night. I struggled with not having administrative support from the hours of 5 p.m. to 7 p.m. until I recognized that my assistant was happy to come in at 10 a.m. and work until I left at 7 p.m. It was difficult to convince the HR people to make an exception to administrative scheduling, but it worked for me. I encourage employers to start small and find a way to make it work for you.

- **Let employees decide what doesn't really matter to you**—This is really a no-brainer when it comes to engaging employees in the business. There are tons of little decisions around administrative matters in your office that are insignificant to you as the employer but are important to your people. For example, simple things like letting employees decide what kind of coffee service to have in the office, engaging them in planning holiday events, seeking their advice on matters through short online surveys, and providing free parking each month to an employee who does something extraordinary. These seemingly small actions engage your people proactively and send a message that you are listening to them and involving them in developing changes and solutions. These small actions yield big dividends.

- **Celebrate family**—Today's young workforce is all about family, and when you ask them to work long hours, sometimes on short notice, it can have a slow and surreptitious effect that undermines their productivity and their attitude about work. As leaders we need to find ingenious ways to include family in the business. Ideas like creating a kid's workday in the office where men and women can bring their children to work for all or part of the day, hosting family events or outings at a theme park, or hosting spouse or significant other luncheons featuring speakers on matters relevant to families. Actions like these can reinforce a culture that says you value the hard work of your people, and that you care about, and are supportive of, their lives outside of work. One of the best decisions I ever made for the group I ran at PwC was to eliminate our annual Christmas party and replace it with a family Christmas party that focused on children. The party, held at my home, was alcohol-free and entirely focused on the family and kids. For example, there was a professional Santa Claus with a photographer taking kid's and family pictures, a separate buffet dinner for children, games and craft projects, balloon artists, a caricaturist drawing family portraits, live Elf shows and storytellers galore. Single staff members were there in force joining in the fun. The event was such a hit that when I retired from PwC, I continued the party, and it is still a major event today. In fact, some of the children who came to the party as five and six-year-olds still show up. The difference is that they drive themselves and often come without their parents. The lesson for me was that anytime you do something for someone's children, they will love you until the day they die. And, at work, they will run through walls for you.

- **Create four-day weekends around big holidays**—Your employees live for weekends. If you want to create a great place to work, try this. For the Fourth of July weekend and for the Christmas/Hanukkah holidays, add Friday as a vacation day before the long weekend starts. The process takes some planning to make sure vital services get covered, but the impact is huge. You'll find that the cost of this extra day is not as significant as you might suspect since most of your people would be taking at least part of that Friday off anyway, and those that were physically present were already mentally on holiday. Actions like this send a message that you care about your people, and more importantly, that you recognize the importance of giving them time off at certain times of year.

- **Be silly and sometimes don't act your age**—Sometimes frivolous things can soften the pressure of hard work for employees of all ages, and remind leaders and employees alike that work should be fun. Try having ice cream or Popsicle parties in the office from time to time to celebrate milestone accomplishments or just for fun. Make your next big meeting extraordinary by bringing in a "cash cube money machine"—a plexiglass enclosure with air blowing and swirling cash bills around inside while an employee tries to catch as many of the bills as they can in sixty seconds. A thousand dollars in $1, $5, and $10 denominations will look like a million dollars in the enclosure. Mix in a few $100 bills for fun. Your people will love it, and it will not cost you the fortune that it looks like. There are hundreds of similar ideas like this one that send a message that we work hard, but we also know how to have fun together. Find the ones that work for you, and relish the silliness.

**Step 3. Create Jedi Knights who serve as role models for others**—I admit that I am a Star Wars junkie. I especially like that exclusive group of well-trained Jedi Knights who use "the Force" as the guardians of peace and justice. If you want to inspire young workers to embrace hard work and commitment, you have to create role models in your organization who live the culture and set the example for others. Create your own group of "Jedi Knights" who are on a quest to become extraordinary and are demonstrating the values you want to instill in your people. Treat these people special and reward them for their significant work and contributions. Reward them openly with bonus compensation. Recognize their accomplishments and create a plan for them to grow personally and professionally. For example, you might create an Executive Development program that is designed for your Jedi Knights to help deepen and broaden their functional expertise, their interpersonal skills, and their involvement in the broader business community.

These are not new ideas; they have been championed by larger companies like General Electric and others that group their employees into A, B, and C divisions. The A employees are the stars and tend to be the workaholics, while the B players are steady workers who do a relatively good job. The C players, of course, are those employees who are not performing up to standard. Managers were encouraged to find ways to turn their B players into As, their C players into Bs, and ultimately to counsel those Cs that could not make the grade out of the company. I always referred to this system as one of Tigers, Horses, and Dogs; you feed the tigers, ride the horses, and shoot the dogs. There has been significant pushback on this system of ranking employees perhaps with good reason since studies have shown that the so-called B players produce about 80% of the work that gets done.

So, why I am suggesting that you create this special group of employees, my Jedi Knights, when the evidence shows that these prima donnas are usually recruited away by other companies and their special treatment tends to antagonize that steady group of B players that you depend on to get things done? I am *not* suggesting that your Jedi Knights are all A players, but should also include a disproportionate number of B players who are setting the example that you want the rest of your workforce to aspire to. They would not be restricted to that handful of "Franchise Players" that fit the A player definition, but would rather be the group that you want to inspire others to work hard, welcome more responsibility, and grow professionally and personally. One of the best ways to accomplish this is to select your Jedi Knights from those employees who are not settling for Average and who are on a demonstrable quest to become Extraordinary. Your selected Jedi Knights will become the role models for the values you want to inspire in your people.

At least three things happen when you take this approach. First, the selected employees will be inspired to do more and to live up to their recognized status. Second, the other employees will be envious and will begin to ask, "How can I become part of this group?" And finally, your people will be pleased when you let them discover that you want them all to join in the quest to abandon Average to become Extraordinary. Role models are powerful tools in motivating employees; create them and use them to inspire others.

### How can you differentiate yourself and become Extraordinary?

Before you conclude that I have gone overboard with pampering young workers with meaningful work, flexible schedules, more weekend days, and popsicles, let's consider the second question we raised in our quest to abandon Average and become Extraordinary by "biting off more than we can chew." My grandmother used to tell me with all her Southern charm that "it's a mighty thin slice of ham that ain't got but one side." Think about it; it will grow on you. Young employees in the workplace clearly have a responsibility to own part of the perception that labels them lazy, entitled, selfish, and totally ambivalent about their work ethic. Just as employers have to redefine what traditional work looks like, Millennials in the workplace have to embrace work not just to find and keep a job, but to be competitive in the marketplace with thousands of smart, educated, and technically savvy workers who look just like them. How do you break out of your homogeneous, look-a-like group and become Extraordinary? How do you embrace hard work and "bite off more than you can chew," while staying true to the guiding light that calls you to avoid becoming a workaholic like your parents. Let me suggest a few ideas.

- **Extinguish the flame of entitlement that burns in your breast**—If you believe the Pew Research and my own personal research, you have to come to the conclusion that the current and future generation of workers, like no generation before them, feel, in their own words, a sense of entitlement. Whether you attribute this attitude to the success and generosity of your parents, the country's changing social agenda, or some complex psychoeconomic reason, the fact remains that young workers have a flame of entitlement that burns in their breast, rarely surfacing overtly, but always lingering just below the point of outward combustion. This attitude is very easy to recognize in others, but is extremely difficult to see in the mirror. Just like the older generation who can't see the entitlements built into the tax code they enjoy—mortgage interest deduction for homeowners, etc.—younger workers can't see the increasing ramification on their work ethic of that built-in sense of entitlement. But it's there and it will impact, ultimately, their success and their quest to become Extraordinary.

So how do you change? First, recognize that it exists and clinically assess how it influences your thinking. Since it is hard to see in the mirror, you will likely have to force yourself to think about the subtle ways in which you expect parents, employers, the government, and others to do things for you or on your behalf. Once you catch a glimpse of how sinister the notion of entitlement is, you then have to face the stark reality that there is a choice to make—you can accept Average, entitlements and all, or you can decide that no one owes you a living and that you alone are responsible for your success. Write this on a piece of paper or a note card: *No one owes me a living; I owe it to myself.* Then post it in a prominent place where you can see it regularly. Reinforce your commitment by discussing it with a mentor or someone you trust. Remember, recognition is at least half the battle.

- **Practice a positive attitude and watch it become contagious**—Psychologists tell us that a positive attitude has significant benefits on almost every level from health, to work, to relationships, and to most human encounters we experience. There is even some research that suggests that our attitude can contribute to physical healing. When you start your day focused on the positive, rather than the negative, you change your "feedback framework." You no longer look for the reasons something won't work; rather, you search for ways you can make it work. You stop worrying about the fear of failure, and start focusing on the potential for success. You become proactive rather than reactive and your encouraging attitude becomes contagious.

The good news is that there is no magic formula for changing negative attitudes into positive ones, nor is there a complicated process required. The most important step you can take is the first one. When you get up in the morning, look in the mirror and tell the person you see that "today is going to be a good day!" Over the next few hours, force yourself, if you must, to treat every encounter with enthusiasm. From the discussion with your Starbucks barista to your greeting to the receptionist in your office, be positive and enthusiastic. Try it for a day and you will be amazed at the impact you have on others, but more importantly on yourself.

You see, attitude is both a choice and an enabler; the more positive you are the more positive you and others will become. You can start this process slowly, but I don't recommend this. If you are aggressive and deliberate in promoting your new positive attitude, the results will be instantaneous. You are not working any harder, you are not breaking a sweat, but the perception you are leaving is profound.

- **Reframe work as learning**—As we discussed earlier, my advice to young people is to make continual learning one of the three principal criteria for staying with your current employer. When you stop learning, it's time to leave. In the meantime, embrace every assignment or project as a learning exercise that is improving your marketability to other employers. You have probably already acknowledged that you will not stay in your current job forever, so aggressively plan for the next one. In case you do decide to stay, your on-the-job education will have put you miles ahead of your competitive coworkers for the next promotion.

- **Think like an owner, not as an employee**—Owners have a different attitude than employees; they think long-term, not short-term. They have a comprehensive view of the business, rather than a silo mentality. They think about all the employees, not just themselves. These are all characteristics of an owner that you can adopt now and mimic as an employee. Embrace your job with an ownership mentality. Learn everything you can about other departments and how they relate to your department, make a plan for your growth with benchmarks that monitor your progress, and, finally, focus on your fellow teammates and what you can do to help them. This ownership attitude will help you embrace your work as a career, not just a job.

- **Study historical role models**—Mark Twain once said, "The harder I work, the luckier I get." There are hundreds of famous people who attribute their success to sheer hard work, from Jeff Immelt, former CEO of General Electric, who reportedly worked hundred-hour work weeks for 24 years, to Mark Cuban, entrepreneur and NBA Dallas Mavericks owner, who did not take a vacation for seven years while he was starting his first business.[101] If you think these heavy work schedules are limited to men, consider the case of Marissa Mayer, the former CEO of Yahoo, who told *Business Insider* that she used to put in 130-hour work-weeks at Google, and she was able to manage that schedule by being strategic about when she slept, when she show-ered, and how often she went to the bathroom.[102] I am not suggesting that you emulate these "workaholics," but I am suggesting that hard work makes a difference. The quest for Extraordinary is long and it is hard. Average is easy. Take the time to study the habits of successful people in all walks of life. What did they do right? What did they do wrong? Build your own schedule and path to success that works for you.

## The Journey to Extraordinary:
## Tips for the Traveler...

On your journey to become extraordinary, how can you embrace hard work and "bite off more than you can chew," while staying true to the guiding light that calls you to avoid becoming a workaholic like your parents? Try these exercises, but remember Average is easy; the quest for Extraordinary is long and hard.

- **Practice a positive attitude**—when you get up in the morning, look in the mirror and say, "this is going to be a great day" and then greet everyone you see for the next four hours with enthusiasm.

- **Think like an owner, rather than an employee**—think long-term and take a comprehensive view of your company. Develop a personal plan for growth and set benchmarks to monitor your progress.

- **Reframe your work as learning**—Make learning one of your three goals at work: 1) learn something new every day, 2) think about how you are improving your marketability, and 3) make sure you are pursuing your personal happiness.

# CHAPTER 9

## The Early Bird Catches the Worm

### The Elegance of Deliberate Patience

The old saying, "The early bird catches the worm," is found in John Ray's *A Collection of English Proverbs* published in 1670. However, speculation is that, since Ray notes that this saying was a proverb in the 17th century, it likely goes back a lot farther than 1670. According to Elyse Bruce, who publishes *Historically Speaking*, "the saying is a translation from the French: "L'avenir appartient à ceux qui se lèvent tôt." Loosely translated, "The future belongs to those who rise early." Similarly, there is an old German saying that translates "The morning hours have gold in their mouths," and an old Latin saying that translates, "Dawn is a friend of the muses."[103] Although it is impossible to identify the author of the Latin version of "the early bird catches the worm," it is known that the Dutch theologian, Desiderius Erasmus Roterodamus (1466-1536) recorded the saying in his book *De Ratione Studii Epistola* which was published in 1513.[104]

While the history of this old saying may lack clarity, its intent, which has passed down for generations by word-of-mouth, is crystal clear and has nothing to do with birds: the individual who is first to work, first at the event, first to market, first with an idea, first with the solution will reap the biggest reward.

But is it really true that "the early bird gets the worm"? In the 1980s, as the technology markets and Silicon Valley were beginning to boom, there was a common sentiment that an entrepreneur or start-up had to be "first-to-market" to be successful. According to Steve Blank, writing in *Business Insider*, the phrase "first-mover advantage" was popularized in a 1988 paper by a Stanford Business School professor, David Montgomery, and his coauthor, Marvin Lieberman. They wrote, "Using this idea (first-mover advantage) to differenti-ate themselves as the hot new Silicon Valley venture capital-ists, some of his former business school students made this phrase their rallying cry. Soon every other venture capitalist was using the phrase to justify the reckless "get big fast" strat-egies of dot-com startups during the internet bubble."[105]

Since the 1980s, the question of whether or not the "first mover," or the "early bird," has a real competitive advantage has been debated by academics, CEOs, business strategists, and bestselling authors. While there are clear advantages to being "first-to-market" in certain situations—where there is limited knowledge of the product or technology or when the required materials are in short supply—there is substantial evidence to suggest that being first is not an advantage, and that, in fact, the second mover will likely be more success-ful. There are hundreds of examples over the last fifty years where the early bird, or first mover, did not get the worm and the company late to the party became the dominate player in their industry. Consider the following examples that are well chronicled in business literature:

- Google was not the first search engine to dominate the internet. In fact, varied sources put Google anywhere from 11th to 21st in entering the search engine market, yet Google now dominates with a market cap of twenty-five billion dollars.[106]

- Facebook trailed both Friendster and Myspace in entering the social media market, but today it dominates the world of social media and the early birds are mere first-to-market relics.[107]

- Netscape was synonymous with the internet in the mid-1990s, but, in 1998, the browser was sold to AOL and, by the year 2000, it was virtually forgotten. The latecomer was Microsoft, who literally conquered Netscape and others with its Internet Explorer.[108]

- Remember the PalmPilot, the first PDA that dominated the

market? Today, Palm struggles to be third or fourth behind the iPhone, Android, and Blackberry.[109]

There are hundreds of examples like these where the "first-to-market" or the "first mover" pioneered a product or technology only to be surpassed and ultimately dominated by the second, third, or even fourth company to enter the market. Examples include Atari vs. Nintendo, Betamax vs. VHS, or even Ford vs. General Motors. While there is irrefutable evidence that the early bird does not always get the worm, the more important questions are whether there are pervasive reasons why there is an advantage to being second or late-to-market, and how can you use that position in your quest to become Extraordinary? Consider the following obvious factors that often create an advantage to being a deliberate follower rather than a pioneer or, as we call them, First Movers:

- First Movers, by definition, create a market, an often very expensive process. Deliberate followers have a chance to refine or redefine the market with their own brand or differentiation.
- Deliberate followers benefit from the market education provided by the First Movers, i.e., the market's customers are better educated.
- Deliberate followers are able to observe the mistakes made by First Movers—and the consequences of those mistakes—

and make course modifications as necessary. They avoid the temptation to rush to market with less than superior products or with product flaws.

Gerald Tellis and Peter Golder, in their book, *Will and Vision: How Latecomers Grow to Dominate Markets*, debunk the widely held myth that "pioneers" dominate the markets they enter. Their study of the results achieved by early leaders across 66 clearly identifiable markets found that "very few market pioneers actually endure as market leaders. In fact, about 64 percent of market pioneers fail, even in the high-tech and emerging new markets. Of those pioneers who do stay in business, only nine percent become leaders of the markets they establish." Tellis and Golder conclude that first-to-market is not the key to sustainable advantage, but, rather "enduring market leaders" are those who are able to harness five key drivers: vision of the broader market, persistence to overcome obstacles, commitment of financial resources, relentless innovation, and effective leveraging of existing assets.[110] These drivers, when taken in concert with the factors discussed above, make a compelling case for the advantages provided the deliberate follower who patiently waits for the optimal time to enter the market. Rather than rush to be first, the deliberate follower sees a market broad enough for more than one competitor, and an opportunity to learn from the initial mistakes of the "early birds." The deliberate follower seizes the moment and brings a refined product or service with innovative improvements and greater visibility of the obstacles that might slow or impede success. The result is likely to be an advantage driven by lower costs, an improved product, and a better sense of market or consumer expectations.

This arguable advantage of the deliberate follower does not mean that the First Mover will never have a competitive edge. In fact, when there are significant barriers to entry or when the life cycle of a product is relatively short, the First Mover has a distinct advantage and will be hard to beat. Across a broad business environment, however, the general optimism expressed by venture capitalists, executives, and business writers that the First Mover will always have a competitive advantage may be over stated. Tellis and Golder concluded that Wall Street and academics who have historically afforded a premium to the companies and individuals positioned to be a First Mover often make flawed assumptions because of three biases: *a survival bias* that tends to focus only on big success stories and ignores the hundreds of failures; *a self-report bias* that focuses only on current market entrants and ignores earlier failed pioneers that predate their knowledge; and the *bias of narrowly-defined markets* that preclude a plethora of similar products that are excluded from their specifically-defined market.[111]

So what does all this discussion around first mover and follower advantage have on aspiring businesspeople and professionals who are striving to break the back of Average and become Extraordinary? While the above discussion is essentially focused on corporate transactions, the concepts are the same for aspiring businesspeople. But you might say, wait Larry, you have been preaching the idea that extraordinary success requires hard work, initiative, acceleration, and innovation, and now you are suggesting that I slow down, pace myself and wait for others to pioneer the way ahead of me? Quite the contrary! What I am suggesting is that you learn the art of deliberate and elegant patience—patience that can help you harness your internal energy and passion, act as an antidote to frustration, and provide you with a strategy for timing and empowering your actions and increasing their efficacy.

If you are like me, however, patience can sometimes feel like the antithesis of aggressive actions aimed at becoming Extraordinary. While biblical and other spiritual literature admonish us to "live with patience and forbearance," patience often feels like the domain of wimps and procrastinators, hardly the stuff that breaks old rules, debunks myths, and plows new paths to extraordinary results. An understandable view, but consider a new paradigm for patience. Dr. Judith Orloff, in her book, *Emotional Freedom*, has an interesting take on patience. She says, "Patience doesn't mean passivity or resignation, but power. It's a kick-ass, emotionally freeing practice of waiting, watching, and knowing when to act." She goes on to say, "Patience has gotten a bad rap for the wrong reasons.

I'm defining patience as an active state, a choice to hold tight until intuition says, 'make your move.' With patience, you're able to delay gratification, but doing so will make sense and feel right."[112]

In your quest to go beyond Average and become Extraordinary, deliberate patience is your ally and will provide the equivalent of the advantages afforded the deliberate follower as discussed above. Specifically, patience as a strategy will help you:

- **Ensure that your actions are driven by thoughtful intellect, rather than impulse and emotions**—We have all been guilty of letting our emotions take control in moments of extreme stress, anger, or frustration only to later regret a spoken word or a hasty decision. Similarly, we have eaten that extra piece of chocolate cake, drank one too many pops, or made a midnight online purchase all driven by momentary impulse. In these and other similar situations, patience and a rational thought process were ambushed by the emotional and impulsive part of our brain.

  Dr. Orloff references research done at Princeton University where volunteers were given the choice of spending money now or saving it for later. While their brains were scanned through magnetic resonance imaging, as they made choices, the researchers found that when a volunteer opted for an immediate spend, the emotional part of their brain was activated and when they chose to wait on spending money, the neocortex, the part of the brain that controls judgment and intellect, was activated. Their conclusion was that there were two separate anatomical brain structures operating, and patience seemed to be more a function of the reasoning rather than the emotional structure. Dr. Orloff sums it up with this thought: "The message to take away when it comes to patience is don't leave it up to emotions. Get in sync with your neocortex by using the gift of reason. Patience doesn't just materialize. You must mindfully plot it out."[113]

At the end of the day, patience is a choice, right? We can decide to pursue immediate results or we can forego the short-term gratification and take a longer-term and more reasoned approach. But what drives that decision and, from a practical standpoint, how do we, in the words of Dr. Orloff, "get in sync with our neocortex"? Kelly McGonigal, PhD, and author of *The Willpower Instinct* sheds some interesting light on the role of the neocortex in helping us invoke patience and reasoning in our decision-making. She notes that "the prefrontal cortex (that section of the brain right behind your forehead) is the part that helps us with things like decision-making and regulating our behavior. Self-control, or willpower, falls under this heading, and thus is taken care of in this part of the brain. Willpower is a response that comes from both the brain and the body, and is a reaction to an internal conflict. You want to do one thing, such as smoke a cigarette or supersize your lunch, but know you shouldn't. Or you know you should do something, like file your taxes or go to the gym, but you'd rather do nothing."[114]

Dr. McGonigal compares our willpower, our ability to be patient and make reasoned decisions, to a muscle that can get exhausted from overuse. Research has shown that we have a finite supply of willpower, and when we are constantly under stress or making decisions purely on gut instinct for short-term gain, we are depleting that supply. Our prefrontal cortex is ambushed, and reason loses the battle to emotional decision-making.

Unfortunately, the consequences of this losing battle are not just immediate and short-term. Consider "The Marshmallow Test" experiment that was conducted by Professor Walter Mischel at Stanford University in the 1960s. Mischel and his researchers brought hundreds of children between the ages of four and five together and individually sat them alone in a private room. The process began by placing a marshmallow on a table in front of the child. The researcher then told the child that he or she had a choice. They could eat the marshmallow in front of them while the researcher left the room, or they could wait until he returned and they would be rewarded with two marshmallows. If they chose to take the first marshmallow, they would not receive a second one. Some kids quickly ate the first marshmallow. Others squirmed and tried to wait but eventually succumbed to the temptation and likewise gobbled it down. Only a few of the children were able to wait the entire time for the double reward.[115]

This experiment was fascinating as well as entertaining, but the real significant change came years later. As the children grew up, the researchers kept track of them and measured their progress and success in a number of areas. What they found was astounding. The kids who had the willpower to wait and get the second marshmallow had less drug and alcohol abuse, higher SAT scores, better health, and generally performed better in a variety of ways. But wait, there is more. The researchers followed each child for the next 40 years and discovered that the kids who waited patiently for the second marshmallow (now adults) succeeded or performed better in every test they measured. The conclusion: the ability to exercise willpower and to delay instant gratification proved to be critical to the kids' future success as adults.[116] The ability to discipline yourself and not succumb to the quick fixes, the emotional ambushes, the anger flare-ups, and the fleeting self-indulgences has a long-term payoff and the benefit is huge. Deliberate patience can be your muse on a lifelong journey from Average to Extraordinary.

- **Deal with frustration and the obstacles it erects on your journey**—We all have a low tolerance for frustration. We are programmed to want instant internet browsing, quick drive-through at our local Chick-fil-A, cars that start with the push of a button, and systems that respond accurately and reliably every time. When any one of these or a host of others don't work, our frustration levels go through the roof. I once had a young manager at PwC tell me in a moment of sheer frustration that "this would be a great job if I didn't have to deal with the clients who hire us, the partners I report to, and the staff I have to supervise." Her comment was tongue-in-cheek, but she had captured the frustration that aspiring leaders invariably face in a fast-paced business environment where they are under extreme time pressures, facing constant deadlines and supporting demanding customers. These roles would be difficult on a normal, routine day, but throw in curveballs from an irate client, a call from your spouse saying the toilet is stopped up, a monthly report showing inaccurately that your department is underperforming, or a call from your teenager's school saying he was caught with marijuana in class today, and suddenly your path is scattered with obstacles, road-blocks, and warning signs that would challenge any business leader's ability to stay calm and patient.

Unfortunately, your frustrations are not limited to your internal psyche. When we get frustrated, unless we can summon our patience, we lash out in anger, give up on folks too quickly, and even damage long-term relationships. Patience, however, is often the last thing on your mind and you know your frustrations will only get worse when you leave the office and face a few hundred drivers who were transformed into raging maniacs when they got in their car and used the seat belt to strap 3,000 pounds of steel to their backside. You are a reasonable person, and, yes, patience is a virtue, but you are on the verge of resurrecting one or more of the seven deadly sins that lay dormant deep down inside. So what do you do? The frustrations are driving you crazy. How do you bring order back to a lopsided day?

The first step is to stop and recognize that your central intelligence system that makes you logical and reasonable, your prefrontal cortex, is being ambushed by emotional drivers that want you to fight back, act hastily, lash out, blame someone and force an immediate outcome. Amazingly, the simple act of recognizing that there is an internal struggle between your emotions and your reason will begin to put the events of the day back into perspective.

Second, focus on the fact that none of these frustrations— the disappointment in your teenager, the upset client, a single monthly statistic, and certainly not a broken toilet— matter in the long-term. They are immediate situational events that in your long journey toward Extraordinary will be gone, and probably, forgotten before you know it.

Take a deep breath and you can feel the control coming back. As Dr. Judith Orloff, in her book *Emotional Freedom*, says, "Patience gives you the liberating breath you've always longed to take."[117] Patience is your ally and together you can beat back those emotional drivers that attack your mind and body.

Finally, prioritize the issues behind your frustrations and solve them one by one. Your intelligent mind is now in control and your actions and solutions are reasoned and deliberate. They may even be delayed for a period of time while you plot a strategy for long-term resolution. Take time to reflect on what happened. Critically evaluate the tension points and triggers around the frustrations you experienced. Now, make a mental note to keep patience near the surface of your intellect. You will no doubt face different frustrations tomorrow, and patience will be there to defend your prefrontal cortex from the emotional onslaught that is sure to come.

- **Improve your mental and physical health**—There appears to be no question among medical doctors and psychologists that people who are patient are generally healthier. The foundation for this apparently proven theory is that impatient people are generally beset by stress and all the health problems that come along with it including heart disease, muscle tension, high blood pressure, labored breathing, and strokes. Psychologists take a similar view. Robert Emmons, Professor of Psychology at the University of California, Davis and Sarah Schnitker, Professor at Fuller Theological Seminary, published a 2007 study showing that patient people have less depression and negative emotions, perhaps, according to the professors, because they can better deal with upsetting or stressful situations.[118]

The researchers, who studied almost 400 undergraduate students, categorized their study of patience into three types: interpersonal patience, hardship patience, and daily hassle patience. It is not surprising that all three categories supported the initial findings that patient people tend to be more mentally stable and have fewer problems with issues like depression. The interpersonal category represents the patience exhibited in dealing with annoying people with calmness and composure. The participants who exhibited this evenhandedness under pressure were found to be more patient with most people and were hopeful and comfortable with their lives. The hardship group included participants who were dealing with the frustration hardships like health issues, unemployment, and financial problems. Similar to the first group, this kind of patience supported higher mental health and was specifically linked to having more hope. Finally, the daily hassle patience participants— traffic jams, long lines, etc.—were generally more satisfied with their lives than the impatient participants.

In 2012, the professors went a step further and ran a patience training camp for 71 undergraduate students. Quoting from their report, "In two weeks, participants reported feeling more patient toward the trying people in their lives, feeling less depressed, and experiencing higher levels of positive emotions. In other words, patience seems to be a skill you can practice, and such practice might bring benefits to your mental health."[119]

- **Make yourself a happier person**—What makes you happy? It's a simple question, but one that needs perspective to answer. After the mandatory response around family and health, the discussion often revolves around things, and our current supply of things may dictate where we are on our self-proclaimed happy quotient. Dr. Ken Harmon, Provost of Kennesaw State University, has studied the characteristics of happy people. His research has concluded that there is one overriding characteristic that happy people possess. Not surprisingly, it is not money or things; these only contribute about 20 percent to happiness. Dr. Harmon's research has concluded that there is one characteristic that overwhelmingly distinguishes happy people from all others—two simple words: Thank You. Happy people are grateful, and consistently convey their gratitude.[120]

There is an interesting correlation between Dr. Harmon's findings and recent studies of patience and the characteristics of patient people. One of the hallmarks of a patient person, in both historical and more recent studies, is the ability or willpower to forego immediate gratification in anticipation of a better future reward. As reported in one study, "Adults who were feeling grateful were also better at patiently delaying gratification. When given the choice between getting an immediate cash reward or waiting a year for a larger ($100) windfall, less grateful people caved in once the immediate payment offer climbed to $18. Grateful people, however, could hold out until the amount reached $30. If we're thankful for what we have today, we're not desperate for more stuff or better circumstances immediately."[121]

More importantly, I have learned that patience can help you be grateful for situations that for some might be stressful or even annoying. Take for example, a morning when someone is thirty minutes late for a breakfast meeting. Patience has taught me that rather than be angry or irritated at my missing guest, I can be extremely thankful for these few unplanned minutes when I can read the newspaper, catch up on unreturned phone calls, or just relax and enjoy the time alone with a cup of coffee. Similarly, when you are stuck in a traffic jam, rather than panic and yell or moan and groan, try being thankful that you have a radio, and that you can relax and let an opera, or Lady Gaga or Garth Brooks soothe your nerves. Patient people are grateful and grateful people are happy. The happiness comes from the contentment of knowing that your life doesn't depend on the stuff you own. It doesn't depend on your current circumstances. Happiness revolves around the relationships you nurture and your ability to be thankful for all the little things.

If you accept that the benefits of deliberate patience are worth consideration, the obvious follow-up question is how you can develop the patience necessary to realize those benefits. The answer is elegant in its simplicity; patience is a learned skill and you simply must practice, practice, and practice. The experts suggest techniques like meditation and deep breathing, revising expectations, and reframing irritants into opportunities. I have a more practical approach. The following are three exercises that I have developed from personal experience over the last few years. They are guaranteed, if practiced frequently, to strengthen your patience quotient and put you more in control of your life and its circumstances. I call them the KO Outburst, the Delta Dilemma, and the MSAL Method. Let me explain and demonstrate.

- **The KO Outburst**—We all, from time to time, struggle to remain cool and collected in the face of annoying people, inadequate service or the number of little grievances we encounter every day. I have a buddy, whose initials are K.O.

and otherwise shall remain nameless, who takes the struggle to a new level and may be the most intense person on the planet. Interestingly, he has been that way for more than 30 years. Normally, he is a pleasant guy in both informal and business circumstances. However, when you put him in a long line, have a golf caddie misread a putt, have an administrative assistant make an error booking an airline reservation, or any similar minor infractions, he is mysteriously transformed from a mild-mannered person into an absolute tyrant. This intelligent, reasonable, and competent businessman cannot overcome the emotional attack that occurs when little things go wrong. I have seen him yell at his assistants and berate waiters in restaurants for late service. At the country club where he is a member, every caddie that I have spoken to confirmed his erratic behavior. Most are smart enough not to reveal their real thoughts, so their standard comment is "yes, he *is* intense."

If I did not know this person, I would think what you are thinking now: this guy is just an "expletive deleted." I actually think the issue is more extensive than that since I see my friend's behavior exhibited every week by lots of other people, if only to a lesser extent. After watching these incidents for years, and concluding that I would never be able to change my friend, I devised my own deliberate exercise designed specifically to strengthen my own patience, and, as importantly, to model for other people how patience can put you in control of difficult or annoying situations.

Here's the exercise. While I don't intentionally look for long lines or other similar situations, I do relish them when they are there. When I encounter this situation, while waiting and others are complaining, I engage a member of my group in conversation about anything positive. I try to get the person talking about him or herself, and then I try to get them to join me in commiserating about the plight of the busy bank teller, the overworked cashier, or the rude behavior of the other people in line. The results are fascinating. It borders on magic when you see and feel the tension dissipate and the stress level fall, both in you and those around you. All the time, I am subconsciously reminding myself that the KO effect has been countered, and in some small way I have put the world back in balance. Try this exercise for yourself; over time, it is a guaranteed way to strengthen your patience.

- **The Delta Dilemma**—The airlines have provided plenty of fodder for the news media and consumers over the last few years, exacerbated by United Airlines forcibly removing a passenger from an aircraft after assigning and placing him in a seat. Generally, the airlines have done a reasonable job in nurturing and managing customer service in their effort to balance the customer experience with profits and shareholder returns, but sometimes process and protocol get in the way. The purpose of the Delta Dilemma is to provide you with another opportunity to enhance and practice patience.

I live in Atlanta, Georgia and, consequently, I fly Delta Air Lines virtually one hundred percent of the time, and have accrued about 2,000,000 miles in the process. (There is an old joke that if you live in the Southeast and die, on your way to Heaven or Hell you will be required to change planes in Atlanta.) During my pre-retirement travels, dealing with the airline as a Platinum SkyMiles customer was a breeze. I was often upgraded, paid no change fees, and generally was treated like I was "kind of a big deal." However, when I retired, and my travel dramatically diminished, I was relegated to the back with stale peanuts unless there was a passenger with an alleged peanut allergy on board—in which case it was stale pretzels. But the source of my most grievous frustration became dealing with Delta agents over changed reservations, differential airfares, and change fees. I was in Albuquerque with my wife and discovered that the airline had initiated nonstop flights from Albuquerque to Atlanta *after* we had arrived there (our original booking was for a return via Salt Lake City). After contacting the airline to inquire about a change in our return flight, I was offended and indignant (and guilty of the now infamous KO Outburst) when I was told that my reservation could certainly be changed, but with a modest cost of one thousand dollars. It was at this moment I realized that three things were happening. First, my blood pressure and stress level was rising in direct proportion to my ever-decreasing patience. Second, I was modeling behavior that just didn't feel right. And finally, I was making no progress, whatsoever, at getting what I wanted.

Remembering the old definition of insanity, I decided to stop banging my head against this proverbial wall and try a different tactic. I decided on a three-pronged approach. First, I would deal with the Delta agent as a person first, and as an airline employee second. Next, I would express my gratitude and thankfulness for their help. And finally, I would use Delta's own customer service standards as my only bargaining chip. Here's the result of my next phone call:

*Larry*: Hello, Diane. Listen I really appreciate you helping me today. How long have you worked for Delta?

*Diane*: Almost sixteen years this month.

*Larry*: Wow. Congratulations! I bet you've seen your share of some strange and interesting folks over the years.

*Diane*: Oh, you wouldn't believe the stories, but it's been fun. How can I help you Mr. Stevens?

*Larry*: Diane, I have a reservation on a return flight from Albuquerque to Atlanta that connects through Salt Lake City. It was the only flight available when I booked it a few months ago. Now I understand there's a direct flight, and my wife and I would like to get on it.

*Diane*: I am happy to see what I can do Mr. Stevens.

*Larry*: Please, Diane, call me Larry.

*Diane*: Larry, can I put you on hold for just a minute?

*Larry*: Sure.

*Diane*: (Several minutes later) Larry, I can make that change, but there is a $150 change fee per ticket and a $350 difference in price between the two fares which is a combined total of $1000 for both you and your wife. Would you like me to go ahead with the change?

*Larry*: Holy Mackerel, that's a lot! I understand it's not your fault, Diane, but I guess you just have to live with the policy. It is interesting though. On the flight out, I listened to your CEO, Richard Anderson talk, on the inflight video, about the importance of frequent travelers and how much Delta values those customers. I used to fly three times a week, I have a couple of million miles, but, since I retired, I don't fly as much, so I guess I no longer meet Mr. Anderson's definition of a valued customer. But I really need to get back to Atlanta sooner than the current flight will arrive, so go ahead and book the new flight.

*Diane:* Larry, can I put you on hold for just a few more minutes?

*Larry:* Sure.

*Diane:* (ten minutes later) Larry, I am so sorry for the long wait, but I went ahead and sent you an email with the new flight information for you and your wife. We want you to know how much we value you as a customer and we have waived both the difference in the fares as well as the change fees. Is there anything else I can do for you this evening?

*Larry:* Diane, you have been marvelous. I really appreciate your time and your interest. Congratulations again. I now know why you are such a valued and long-term employee of Delta. Have a great evening.

Now you might think that this was an isolated incident or that I just got lucky. Not the case. I have changed tickets numerous times since then and I have never paid a change fee or a price differential. In every instance, I have invoked the Delta standard for customer service—"we value our customers"—and every time it works. More importantly, I adhere to my three-part plan: Connect with the agent as a person; express gratitude; and, finally, hold the airline to their own standard of service. The act of saving a few dollars on airline tickets is important, but not nearly as important as the intangible benefits.

Try the Delta Dilemma, not just with airlines, but with all your vendors or service providers. It will eliminate stress in your life, build your reservoir of patience, and boost your self-confidence for your next encounter. And it might even save you some money!

- **The MSAL Method**—Have you ever felt overwhelmed and frustrated by an organization's bureaucracy and the innumerable forms and obstacles that are erected seemingly to slow the process to a snail's pace and to most certainly and insidiously drive you crazy? We have all experienced the frustration of corporate, institutional, and governmental processes designed for some subtle purpose that is hard to detect, and whose navigation is guaranteed to raise your blood pressure and test even the "patience of Job." I have a friend, Dr. Mike Salvador, retired Director of Executive Education and Senior Lecturer at Kennesaw State University, MSAL for short (there's a story behind the acronym), who has taught me the art of mastering the bureaucratic malaise. Mike had a simple approach for solving the problem of administrative beadledom. He simply reframed every problem or obstacle as a challenge. Rather than fight the administrators or complain about any seemingly endless set of roadblocks, he saw every situation as an opportunity for his intellect, creativity, and cleverness to not only plow through the morass of arcane policies and procedures, but to actually improve the process for himself, his colleagues, and the University. The mindset conversion from problem to challenge redirected Mike's attention from the problem and focused his energy on the solution.

This attitudinal change process had three significant effects and at least two ancillary consequences. First, Mike was stress free in dealing with a process that would drive the normal person literally "up a wall." Not only was he stress free, he was energized, enthusiastic, and empowered in his search for the elusive solution. Second, Mike prided himself on ultimately building a better mousetrap; his solutions have, in some cases, been the catalyst for changes to policies and procedures and have raised awareness of the need for the reengineering of attendant processes and protocols. Finally, Mike reinforced to himself, and those around him, the power of patience and the superiority of reason over emotion.

The ancillary benefits of Mike's approach were unintended, but just as potent. First, his nonconfrontational and collaborative style put the normally defensive administrators at ease, and, over time, he built and nurtured relationships that fostered solution-oriented discussions. As importantly, he turned the beadledom from departmental enemies to cooperative allies. The result: Mike built a cadre of people who took his call on the first ring, were not threatened by his presence, and who believed that he just might actually care about them as breathing people. Guess what? He actually did. And there is more. The University administration—President, Provost, and Deans—heard the rumors of Dr. Salvador's ability to navigate the systems and find that one point on a wavy line that people could gather around. They regarded him as a valuable resource, and when there was a sticky problem or a strategic issue with lots of moving parts, Mike was their "go to person."

I have asked Mike the secret to his success. In his "aw shucks" manner, he talks about the importance of methodical and deliberate patience and his inescapable conclusion that most people, just like him, only want to do the right thing—you just have to show them the way while also demonstrating respect for the position in which the status quo has put them.

Here is the MSAL exercise. The next time you are faced with a bureaucratic nightmare, bask in the opportunity to make a difference rather than just a point. Reframe the problem in the context of its solution and use your creativity to solve it. Your patience will grow exponentially, and you will marvel at the triumph of reason and logic over emotion.

## The Early Bird vs. The Night Owl

A discussion about patience and the question of whether or not the "early bird gets the worm" would not be complete without some mention of the often-debated Early Bird vs. the Night Owl. Who is more productive or successful, the early riser who may get up as early as 5 a.m. and go to bed very early that night, or the late sleeper who goes to bed in the wee hours of the morning and sleeps until 8 or 9 a.m. the same day? In other words, was founding father Ben Franklin's well known saying, "Early to bed, early to rise, makes a man healthy, wealthy, and wise" truth or myth?[122]

Lynn Stevens is a lawyer, and I have been married to her for over 50 years. For all those years, she has risen from our bed between 4:30 and 5:30 a.m., if not earlier. She is a text-book early bird who likes to be in bed by 10:00 p.m. every night. She is smarter than me, a multitasking master, a highly productive lawyer who rarely loses a case, and a caring person with a servant's heart. But you have to admit, she is a little weird, right? How can anyone consistently get up that early and function at all? So I was surprised when I learned that Presidents George Bush (41 and 43); Howard Schultz, former Starbucks CEO; Tim Cook, Apple CEO; Jeff Immelt, former GE CEO; former Secretary of State, Condoleezza Rice; and a whole host of similarly successful people all wake up between 3:45 and 5:00 a.m. Notwithstanding their success and, in many cases, celebrity, I still don't get it. I go to bed after midnight every night and get up in the morning when necessary, but usually after 7:00 or 8:00 a.m. I do, from time to time, long to be one of those early risers who is at the gym by 5:30 a.m., catches up on emails before the phones start to ring, and reads three newspapers by 9:00 a.m. I have even tried to get into this early morning routine more than a few times over the last twenty years with abject failure.

For a moment, I actually began rethinking the thesis for this book; maybe some of the old myths like "The early bird catches the worm" really are true. Then my research led me further. Winston Churchill, the former prime minister of the United Kingdom, apparently loved to manage the first part of his day from his bed; former U.S. President Barack Obama is reportedly a major night owl; Charles Darwin apparently always slept in; and a host of others including Carl Jung, J.R.R Tolkien, and Gustave Flaubert were all reportedly night owls. Excuse me, I almost forgot Elvis—the King of the night owls.[123] So let's dismiss the myth that night owls are lazy or can't be successful. In fact, the scientific evidence around the comparison of night owls, or late sleepers, and early birds, larks, or early risers, is both fascinating and intriguing. A few interesting facts and observations cited by psychologists and scientists are worth noting:

- **It is genetics, not work habit, that establishes whether we are early birds or night owls**—We all have a unique chronotype which governs our inclination to sleep at a particular time during a 24-hour period. This 24-hour period is referred to as our circadian clock or circadian rhythm, a cycle that tells our bodies when to sleep, when to get up, when to eat and governs other physiological processes. According to Frederick Brown, professor of psychology at Penn State University, "people span the range of those who are very early risers to very late setters, and this is genetically determined. If you're a morning-type person, you can't become an evening type and vice-versa." Actually, according to Dr. Brown, about half the population are in an intermediate range and can easily get up an hour or two earlier and go to bed an hour or two later without much of a problem. The remaining population is about evenly split between night owls and early birds, with the extreme early risers making up only one percent of the population.[124] The takeaway for you: You can't change who you are. Accept your genetics and make it work for you. If you are unsure as to whether you are an early bird or a night owl, there is a questionnaire in the Appendix that will help you figure it out.

- **Are early birds or night owls healthier, wealthier, or wiser?**—Numerous studies have been conducted by universities and research groups in both the United States and

Europe around this question. The results are varied, with the preponderance of evidence not overwhelming either way, but at least one study of 356 early birds and 318 night owls suggested that night owls had the greater incomes. The same study concluded also that both groups showed no significant differences in either cognitive tests or self-reported health issues.[125]

- **Most studies have concluded that night owls tend to have higher intelligence**—According to *Psychology Today*, one such study completed by Satoshi Kanazawa, an evolutionary psychologist at the London School of Economics found that "young American children who were more intelligent grew up to be more nocturnal than their less intelligent counterparts." Kanazawa also carried out extensive research into the connection between sleep patterns and intelligence. Kanazawa theorizes that "whilst our ancestors 10,000 years ago used to rise and fall with the sun much like our animal friends following their circadian rhythm, advances in technology have allowed intelligent brains to ignore that impulse and search for stimulation late at night."[126] I will let you draw your own conclusions with respect to the competitive intelligence between early birds and night owls. I know at least one night owl named Lynn Stevens who will likely take issue with Dr. Kanazawa's findings.

So there are mixed reviews as to the validity of old Ben Franklin's sage advice. I will leave it to you to determine which chronotype—morningness or eveningness—you are and, in that role, whether you are smarter, richer, or healthier than all the contra-chronotype people with whom you hang.

**The Journey to Extraordinary:
Traveling Tips...**

Learn the art of deliberate and elegant patience—Patience that will help you harness your internal energy and passion, act as an antidote to frustration, and provide you with a strategy for timing and empowering your actions and increasing their efficacy.

- **Take the antidote for the KO Outburst**—Relish stressful situations around other people and engage the stressed out individuals in a refocused and positive dialogue. You will be amazed at how well it works.

- **Master the MSAL Method**—Reframe every administrative problem or obstacle you face as a challenge requiring a solution. This simple attitudinal shift will lower your stress level, improve relationships with the beadledom in your life, and might actually result in you building a better mouse-trap.

- **Practice saying "Thank You" regularly**—Happy people know how to say thank you even when circumstances are difficult or unexpected. Be thankful for the little things.
- **Take the Questionnaire in Appendix II**—Embrace your chronotype, be it early bird or night owl; make it work for you.

# CHAPTER 10

# The Love of Money is the Root of All Evil

## Embrace Ambition

"The love of money is the root of all evil"—a powerful statement that evokes a host of emotions, some positive, but most negative. It is a warning that, at worst, conjures images of the biblical rich man and his impending doom to hell, fire, and damnation; and, at best, reminds us of the dire consequences of serious misplaced priorities. There are, indeed, religious overtones to the statement and they are not limited to the Christian and Jewish faiths. In fact, every one of the world's major religions warns the faithful of losing perspective and even their lives in the pursuit of financial gain.

I am not ready to challenge the accuracy or veracity of written scripture, regardless of one's religious affiliation, but I do think that, for the last few hundred years, the love of money has been given a bad rap. In fact, the original admonition is often misquoted as "money (not the love of money) is the root of all evil." Let me give you a different perspective on the importance of money; defend your ambitious pursuit of financial gain, and reconcile it with the mandates of your moral and ethical compass.

## The Importance of Money

People with money make things happen. It is the currency that drives our global economy, and it influences virtually every aspect of our lives. We pursue it relentlessly during our working careers and hopefully save enough to retire comfortably. Money is obviously important to us individually because it provides the basic essentials for living, and affords the opportunity to travel, support family, and enjoy a reasonable lifestyle. On a broader level, money has far-reaching implications that transcend our routine receipt of paychecks and payment of bills, but nonetheless are just as critical to success in both our personal and professional lives. Money is the lubricant for a global financial economy that knows no borders, fuels the expansion of governments, provides a marketplace for corporate goods and services, funds research and development for new technologies, and feeds the ever-growing and insatiable need for capital in both public and private markets. Money makes medical breakthroughs possible. Money defends the United States against foreign enemies. Money educates our children. Money entertains us through sports teams, arenas, and Hollywood. Money funds our religious institutions. In short, money impacts every aspect of our lives and everything we do.

Now before you start warming the coals to sacrifice me on the altar to the gods of "Meaningful Life" and "Work-Life-Balance," let me explain. Most boomers had a workaholic lifestyle and, at some point near the end of their careers, they realized that money alone cannot make you happy. The data is clear on that point. The accumulation of wealth as a goal is misguided and usually ends in disappointment, even if the goal is achieved. Perhaps the best illustration of this is the workaholic generation of investment bankers portrayed in the 1987 movie *Wall Street*, when Gordon Gekko declared with authority that "Greed is good!"[127] The movie depicts all that is bad with a generation of business leaders who were obsessed with making money at any cost. But it is also a legacy of the financial system that made access to capital ubiquitous in this country. In your journey to break the bonds of Average and become Extraordinary, you cannot ignore the need for money, and you cannot ignore the people who can give you access to that money.

## The Importance of Knowing People with Money

Ever notice that people with money always seem to be in a leadership role whether at an industry trade meeting, the

Chamber of Commerce, the local Rotary club, the First Baptist Church, the community Synagogue, the local country club, or even the dreaded neighborhood association? Is it simply because they are rich and bought their way in? Perhaps, but it is more likely because they have accrued influence that gives them both credibility and power; a level of influence they have developed through demonstrable leadership that causes others to gravitate toward them. The influence they wield is often the result of the power of the position they hold, and other times it is the result of the power of their personality. Either way, these are people that you cannot ignore. And that brings us to a cardinal rule I want you to commit to memory. The rule is simple: *You can never, ever know enough people with money or access to money.*

Now the first reaction to this simple rule is that true relationships cannot be based on money, and, quite frankly, many of you are offended that someone would even suggest that relationships start with money. Most people, if asked publicly, will tell you that they are not driven by money; and that money is not the most important thing in their lives—not in their jobs, their marriage, their careers, or any of their relationships. Remember where we started. The Bible teaches that "the love of money is the root of all evil." Right? So why am I so focused on access to capital and money? The reason is simple. Your personal business success will depend, at some point, on access to capital and on you having relationships with people that control that access.

In the business community, whether we are willing to admit it or not, access to capital and, hence, money, is the key to starting, promoting, progressing, and often completing business initiatives. Your entrepreneurial idea, your brilliant business solution, or your innovative suite of products will never go beyond your vivid imagination if you can't get them to market. And you can't get them to market without money. Today, capital for entrepreneurial ideas and small to middle market businesses is available and fairly simple to find if you spend the time to understand and develop a relationship with the network of capital that exists in virtually every city in the United States. The caveat, of course, is that the economy will always dictate the availability of capital, both debt and equity, and, in a time of deep recession, capital becomes harder to find and often is not available.

## Universal Access to Capital— A Short History Lesson

The doctrine of universal capital has not always been the case. Historically, access to capital was the domain of Wall Street, and only the most sophisticated companies and financial engineers had easy access. Over the last two decades, this has changed, reinforcing why the number and quality of your personal business relationships are so important. Remember the rule. It bears repeating: "You can never, ever know enough people with money or access to money."

Before the 1980s, capital formation was the sole domain of Wall Street and the large investment banking houses led by Goldman Sachs, Lehman Brothers, Solomon Brothers, and a handful of other "white shoe" firms. There were always wealthy people who made private investments, but this private equity existed only in rarefied places and was generally invisible to the business community at large. While access to capital began to significantly expand for the first time in the 1970s, primarily linked to the growth of the real estate industry that saw construction being financed from nontraditional and foreign sources, the real breakthrough in the regional availability of capital began to occur after the recession in the early 1980s.

Around 1983-1984, the concept of venture capital was growing in popularity throughout the United States in part because of the bullish stock market, but more importantly because of the surge in entrepreneurship and the huge leaps in technology that presented alternative investments to both institutional and personal investors. During this period, personal and ad hoc venture investing formalized into actual "venture funds" that attracted money from institutions and wealthy individuals and invested in early-stage technology companies. A few of these ventures are the stuff of legends like Apple

Computer and Microsoft, but most of them were dismal failures because the entrepreneurs and, in many cases, the venture funds failed to realize that money invested in product development is wasted if there are not sufficient funds to get the products to market. The good news of this era, however, was that the venture capital business survived, fed by the handful of phenomenal successes of the technology boom of the late 1980s and early 1990s, and the ensuing greed of investors who were tired or bored with making normal Standard & Poor's returns in the stock market. Venture capital opened the door to, and in some cases morphed into, leveraged buyout funds, private equity funds, and eventually hedge funds. Investors, both large and small, realized the power behind identifying innovative start-up ventures or under-performing companies and providing them funding to either bring their new ideas to market or accelerating their growth through new business strategies.

While the stories of the magnificent successes and the miserable failures of this era in American business are well-documented—RJR Nabisco's $25 billion leveraged buyout, Michael Milken and Drexel Burnham Lambert's junk bond financing, the rise of KKR and other private equity funds, etc.—the more sweeping and significant change was the rise of what I call the "financial engineering middle class." Heretofore, access to capital in American business had been generally limited to the aforementioned elite group of sophisticated financial engineers and Wall Street investment bankers who brokered financing transactions and protected the closed door to capital like it was Fort Knox. When Michael Milken and Drexel pioneered the junk bond (less than investment grade debt), the business community-at-large had little idea that the aristocratic financial engineering community was about to become a middle class. A financial engineering middle class emerged that was comprehensive, and it spawned an entire industry of bankers, lenders, advisors, brokers, accountants, and consultants who considered themselves qualified to provide access to both private and public capital.

A case in point is the story of a young 33-year-old accountant working as head of strategic planning for a middle market public company in 1986. This woman walked into my office one bright summer day and stated, rather confidently, that she wanted to buy the manufacturing division of her company that was being sold as the company strategically realigned its businesses. In response to my question, the woman confessed that she had no money and virtually no assets that could be collateral for financing. Furthermore, she had no experience in running a company. Ultimately, the purchase of the manufacturing division was consummated with the entire purchase price, including deal fees, financed 100% by Westinghouse Credit Corporation. This is just one example of bold entrepreneurs and businesspeople who were finding access to capital as the mergers and acquisitions business abandoned its aristocratic Wall Street breeding to do deals on Main Street USA. The cottage industries of consultants and bankers supporting the deal business blossomed into big and highly profitable departments in law firms, accounting firms, banks, consulting firms, and insurance companies.

This flurry of activity was dampened during the recession of 1989-1993, but the poor economy on Wall Street fostered an army of B and C investment bankers who formed their own M&A businesses or joined small boutique firms which were touting that they brought Wall Street talent to their existing hometown relationships. As a result, the number of professionals and businesspeople who arguably could provide some access to capital was growing exponentially, and other businesspeople who had some level of access to these professionals was growing even faster. At the same time, traditional regional banking institutions were forming investment banking departments or looking for boutique M&A shops to acquire, thereby accelerating the number of relatively unsophisticated professionals and investment banker trainees with a hands-on education in helping middle market companies find equity and debt financing.

As the economy gained strength and momentum in the mid-1990s, it was common for the large accounting firms to also begin forming investment banking businesses and promising clients that they could combine Wall Street talent with Main Street service. Similarly, law firms formed corporate finance departments that touted their ability to not only handle the legal chores, but also provide one-stop shopping by identifying sources of both debt and equity financing for their clients. By the spring of 2001, the frenzy was still roaring at a rapid pace, but there were dark clouds on the horizon. The disaster of September 11 did not cause the economic recession, but it did serve to bring immediate reality and recognition to the excesses that had built up during the technology boom of the 1990s. The downturn also had a sobering effect on the availability of capital. Lenders that were providing senior debt financing at amounts equal to 10 and 12 times earnings before interest, taxes, depreciation and amortization (EBITDA) were suddenly loath to provide the same financing at greater than 3 or 4 times EBITDA.

The impact on the availability of capital from the technology bust and the tragedy of the twin towers was exacerbated by the corporate cockroaches that appeared in the form of Enron, Worldspan, etc., during 2001-2003. Confidence in American business and the financial markets appeared to crumble as accounting scandal after accounting scandal was uncovered. Even the seemingly invincible accounting firm, Arthur Andersen, was forced out of business. During this financial storm, lenders, private equity funds, financial institutions, and corporations alike hunkered down with a bunker mentality. Most private equity funds turned their attention to managing existing portfolio companies, while corporate boards began to rethink governance and managerial accountability.

The storm continued unabated until the middle of 2003 when the economy finally began to recover. The tumultuous twenty-year period from 1983 to 2003, with its roller coaster ups and downs, saw the rise and fall—and subsequent resurrection—of junk bonds, the rise of sophisticated derivative financial instruments, and the emergence of private equity as a major financial force. More importantly, it eventually spawned the expansion of capital sources and the creation of new regional and national financial referral networks.

## The Secret to Accessing Capital

Today, regional capital sources, often with global financial support and related referral networks, provide businessmen and women the opportunity to identify and obtain capital more easily than any other time in the country's history. The secret is in knowing either the people that control the capital, or the people who have access to the people that control the capital. And thanks to the regionalization of capital that has occurred and continued to expand over the last twenty years, the access points are virtually at every businessman or woman's doorstep. They could be the bankers in your town, the lawyers in the myriad of big and small law firms, the businesspeople you meet at the gym, the accountants in both the "Big Four" national firms and similar regional firms, your insurance professionals, the consultants who live in your neighborhood, and any number of other people who have the ability to introduce you to sources of money or people with access to money. They can be found at industry trade meetings, churches and synagogues, the local Chamber of Commerce, your kids' school and sporting events, and, yes, even at the dreaded neighborhood association.

A case in point: A development officer at a major university in Atlanta once told me he could get me a meeting with one of the three vice chairs of General Electric Corporation. I was surprised and, quite frankly, shocked at the offer, but I was overwhelmed by the suggestion that this "academic type" had a relationship with one of the three top officers of arguably the best managed company on the planet. After accepting his gracious offer, I inquired as to how he knew the GE officer. His answer may be as surprising to you as it was to me.

It turns out that the development officer is invited to an annual holiday party in a friend's neighborhood, the same neighborhood where the GE executive lived. The GE executive travels all the time and while his wife knew everyone in the neighborhood, he knew very few people. The development officer had struck up a conversation with the executive at the first party a few years back, and, every year since, the two share one thing in common: neither one knows any other people in the neighborhood. The one chance meeting several years ago had created a relationship that allowed the "academic," who was clearly not in the executive's corporate hierarchy or pay category, access to someone who had both money and access to money. And, interestingly enough, it came through an encounter at a routine neighborhood association meeting. An interesting story, but what's the takeaway? As an aspiring business leader, entrepreneur, or professional, access to capital is at your fingertips. The critical step that you can take is to ensure that you put yourself in a position to meet these people with power and influence? Why? Because you can never know enough people with money or access to money.

## Is Money Really the Root of All Evil?

Hopefully, I have established the importance of money and access to capital in your pursuit to become Extraordinary. But have we sufficiently addressed our original question, or at least the question that must be implicit in the original perception that money is the root of all evil? Is there no middle ground? Is the accumulation of wealth always an evil concept, or can we reverse engineer the concept to achieve our objectives and remain true to our principled belief that Gordon Gekko was wrong; that, indeed, greed is not good, but neither is the ambition to make money and grow wealth bad?

I have always been intrigued by Napoleon Hill and his 1937 book *Think and Grow Rich* which lays out thirteen principles for accumulating wealth. In response to the question of how a person can accumulate money, and perhaps in defense of his unbridled ambition, Hill penned the following words that are worthy of your consideration: "We often hear politicians proclaiming the freedom of America when they solicit votes, but seldom do they take the time or devote sufficient effort to the analysis of the source or nature of this 'freedom.' Having no axe to grind, no grudge to express, no ulterior motives to be carried out, I have the privilege of going into a frank analysis of that mysterious, abstract, greatly misunderstood 'something' which gives to every citizen of America more blessing, more opportunities to accumulate wealth, and more freedom of every nature than may be found in any other country. The name of this mysterious benefactor is capital! Capital consists not alone of money, but more particularly of highly organized, intelligent groups of men who plan ways and means of using money efficiently for the good of the public, and profitably to themselves. These groups consist of scientists, educators, chemists, inventors, business analysts, publicity men, transportation experts, accountants, lawyers, doctors, and both men and women who have highly specialized knowledge in all fields of industry and business. They pioneer, experiment, and blaze trails in new fields of endeavor. They support colleges, hospitals, public schools, build good roads, publish newspapers, pay most of the cost of government, and take care of the multitudinous detail essential to human progress. Stated briefly, *the capitalists are the brains of civilization*, because they supply the entire fabric of which all education, enlightenment, and human progress consists."

Hill went on to say that, "Money without brains is always dangerous. Properly used, it is the most important essential of civilization." [128] Implicit in his observation is the understanding that there must be ethical bounds and constraints around how we accumulate and spend money. So what are those ethical bounds that will keep our desire to accumulate wealth from becoming an unhealthy obsession? Let me offer three ideas that will keep your ambition in proper perspective in your quest to become Extraordinary.

- **Stay relentlessly focused on purpose rather than stuff**— It never ceases to amaze me how much "stuff" we collect, even as moderately affluent people. Whether it is antique furniture, classic cars, celebrity autographs, Fabergé eggs, or simple baseball cards, we just can't seem to get enough. The more disposable income we generate, the more stuff we think we need. The peril, of course, is that we get attached to the stuff and ultimately to the money we need to buy the stuff.

  I encourage young people that I mentor to stay focused on your real purpose in life, your job, and your marriage, and appreciate that, 25-30 years from now, the stuff you have accumulated will be meaningless. I encourage them to start keeping a daily journal in leather-bound books that chronicles their daily or weekly experiences over a long period of years, a journal that captures with demonstrable evidence who they were and what mattered to them. The ultimate payoff is when they are able to pass along that historical legacy of their life to their children. Trust me, your children would rather have journals chronicling your life than your old sofa or other "stuff" that you have collected.

Arthur C. Brooks, in an article published in the New York Times, *Abundance Without Attachment*, admonishes his readers to "get to the center of the wheel." He says, "In the rose windows of many medieval churches, one finds the famous 'wheel of fortune', or Rota Fortuna. Following the wheel's arm around, one sees the cycle of victory and defeat that everyone experiences throughout the struggles of life. At the top of the circle is a king; at the bottom, the same man as a pauper. Everyone was supposed to remember that each of us is turning on the wheel. One day, we're at the top of our game. But from time to time, we find ourselves laid low in health, wealth, and reputation. Every victory seems an exercise in futility, because soon enough we will be back at the bottom."[129]

The theologian Robert Barron, in response to the vicious cycle of the wheel's victory and defeat was quoted as saying, "The early church answered this existential puzzle by placing Jesus at the center of the wheel. Worldly things occupy the wheel's rim. These objects of attachment spin ceaselessly and mercilessly. Fixed at the center was the focal point of faith, the lodestar for transcending health, wealth, power, pleasure and fame—for moving beyond mortal abundance."[130]

The takeaway for us is to avoid holding on to the worldly stuff that rides on the outer rim of the wheel. Rather, make sure your foundational purpose and truth are at the center of your wheel and keep that as your focus.

- **Collect stories, not possessions**—Everybody has a story to tell. In your efforts to put yourself in position to meet people with money and access to money, you have an incredible opportunity to listen to and learn from the stories of wealthy people that you meet.

I recently played golf at the Sage Valley Golf Club in Graniteville, South Carolina, only a short distance from Augusta National, and had the pleasure to meet and sit with the owner and founder of the club, Mr. Weldon Wyatt. Mr. Wyatt, a courtly gentleman in his sixties, was gracious and accommodating as he made sure that our experience on the golf course was good and that we had "been taken care of." Rumor had it that Mr. Wyatt wanted to join Augusta National but the invitation never came. Rather than whine, the real estate developer found about 10,000 acres near Aiken, South Carolina and built a magnificent course to rival Bobby Jones' course not far away. He apparently even recruited a number of the Augusta National caddies to join him at the new club.

Curt Sampson, in his book *A Vision, Not a Blueprint: Weldon Wyatt and Sage Valley*, tells the story that, as a young real estate developer, Wyatt had built an early Walmart Store in Bluefield, Virginia. The Walmart store sat close to the city water main, so Wyatt, as the developer, dug an expensive trench and laid a connecting water line pipe with the cost to be offset by future fees for anyone who tapped into it. A few years later, Wyatt Development received an unexpected check for $154,000 from the city of Bluefield. As Curt Sampson recalls, the conversation went something like this: "What do I do with this?" asked Wyatt's controller. "Send half of it to Walmart," Wyatt said, "they paid for half of that pipe in their rent." Unaccustomed to receiving money out-of-the-blue from its developers, Walmart returned the check again and again. Wyatt sent it back again and again, and, finally, over time convinced Walmart that the $77,000 check belonged to them. "I pride myself on keeping my word," was apparently the last mention of this by Mr. Wyatt. As the story goes, at the next Walmart real estate committee meeting where construction projects were matched with and allocated to builders, Sam Walton said, "Give all those to Weldon; he's the only honest developer I know."[131]

Would Weldon Wyatt have become a multi-millionaire, and

the owner of Sage Valley, if he had never sent the $77,000 to Walmart, that is, if his ethics had allowed him to keep the check and chalk it up to his own savvy business skills? Maybe, but you will never convince Weldon Wyatt of that. The takeaway for your journey to Extraordinary is simple. Honesty matters; always do the right thing. And you just might create a story that someone else will hear and add to their collection.

- **Develop an attitude of generosity**—While we are discussing ideas for keeping ambition and money in perspective on your trek to Exceptional, generosity is not always about money. It is much deeper than that. Generosity is a frame of mind that governs not only dollars that you may contribute to charitable causes, but also the investments you make in developing business and personal relationships.

Generosity serves a three-fold purpose on your journey. First, it provides a grounding mechanism that serves as a reminder of how far you have come and where you have come from. Several years ago I had a client from deep South Georgia who became highly successful and wealthy in the temporary staffing business. I asked him what the folks back home thought of his success and he was quick to say, "Larry, when I go back to South Georgia, I am nothing but that little, runny-nose boy. You have to always remember how to go back home." He's right. You stay grounded when you can remember where you came from and who you are.

Secondly, generosity can put your whole life in perspective. Charles Dickens told the story of Ebenezer Scrooge in his novel, *A Christmas Carol*. Scrooge's partner, Jacob Marley had recently died and he appeared as a ghost in Scrooge's dream one night. Marley was shackled in chains and was bemoaning the tortures of the afterlife when Scrooge reminded him "But Jacob, you were a good man of business." Marley answered, "Yes, but Ebenezer, mankind was my business. Benevolence was my business. My trade was but a drop in the comprehensive ocean of my business."[132] Dickens's story is regaled as a Christmas story, but, in fact, it is a story of redemption and a reminder to us that there is a greater purpose to our lives than earnings releases, EBITDA, and balance sheets. As Henry David Thoreau once said, "a man is measured not by what he possesses, but what he gives away."[133]

Finally, generosity is a proactive, demonstrable act of gratitude. It is recognition that you are thankful for those that have made your success possible. Generosity is not simply the donation of money to charitable causes; it is an attitude of service to others that creates a sense of self accomplishment and fulfillment that cannot be duplicated. I was once at a dinner with a group of businesspeople where Ted Turner, the founder of CNN Cable News and a variety of other companies, delivered a speech on philanthropy. Ted was asked what caused him to give away so much money. He responded, "Well, I gave away the first five million and it just felt so good, that I had to give another twenty-five million."[134] Ted went on to challenge others to recognize the obligation to give back to the community that was responsible for their success. This attitude is not limited to the Ted Turners, Bill Gates, or Warren Buffets of the world. There are, in your community, nameless individuals who have given hundreds, thousands, and even millions of dollars anonymously in recognition of their gratitude for the country and community that made their success possible. It is those people who are demonstrable proof that there can be symmetry between the accumulation of wealth and the greater good; that the love of money is not necessarily the root of all evil.

## The Journey to Extraordinary:
## Tips for the Traveler...

Remember just three things:

- **You can never know enough people with money or access to money**—Money makes things happen and regardless of whether you are a businesswoman, a professional, a preacher, a doctor or a factory worker, access to money will help you accomplish your objectives.

- **Stay relentlessly focused on purpose rather than stuff**—Stay focused on the glass balls that will break—family, God, friends—and let the rubber balls—work, hobbies, stuff—bounce along.

- **Collect stories, not possessions**—Study the stories of successful people in your community who are happy and fulfilled. Learn their secrets and put them to work for you. Find a young person and mentor them on what you have learned.

# EPILOGUE

## It's a Sorry Dog Who Won't Wag His Own Tail

### Tell Your Story

A friend of mine, a politician and part-time farmer in South Georgia, was always advising his colleagues and business associates to be more aggressive in promoting their agendas and programs. He was fond of saying, "It's a sorry dog who won't wag his own tail." I always assumed that my friend, in his inimitable southern slang, created this saying only to discover a few years later that it was from the song "Poor Dog," written by the singer, Little Richard. Little Richard's version went like this:

> *Self-preservation is the first law of nature*
> *Above the rules of the one who made you*
> *The good Lord helped those who helped themselves*
> *Look at number one before you help somebody else*

*It's a mighty poor captain, can't sail his own ship*
*And it's a poor, poor actor, can't read his own script*
*It's a poor foundation, can't hold up a house*
*It's a mighty poor cat, can't even catch a mouse*

*Cause it's a poor dog*
*Now, it's a poor dog*
*It's a poor dog*
*Who can't wag his own tail*[135]

Regardless of the source, the message is clear. You need to be willing to tell your own story, a story that chronicles your own journey toward Extraordinary, regaled with its magnificent successes and fraught with its miserable failures. My experience over the last forty years in business is that extraordinary people are good storytellers, and that should raise at least three questions in your mind: why tell a story, what constitutes a good story, and what makes a good storyteller? Let's address them one by one.

## Why tell a story?

The simple truth is that everyone loves a story. We grew up listening to stories being read to us as children; we were enthralled by stories being told to us at bedtime by our parents. They capture our imagination and they are memorable—sometimes for a lifetime.

When my grown children were less than five years old, I created a series of stories about two imaginary kids named Bunky and Bimbo who were also five years old. This imaginary duo explored forests, climbed trees, and escaped mischief that was of their own doing. A few years ago, my daughter and her mother were discussing the stories and reminiscing about Bunky and Bimbo and their adventures as "elephants." I interrupted them to make the point that Bunky and Bimbo were not elephants; they were five-year-old human children. I was amazed and flabbergasted when, after vehemently arguing, they convinced me that they believed the imaginary duo was really a pair of elephants. The point is not that my children had wild imaginations, or that my ability to communicate the difference between people and elephants might be suspect; but rather, that after thirty years, my daughter remembered every Bunky and Bimbo story in vivid detail. She is no different than you or any of us. Stories touch us emotionally and often leave an indelible mark on our psyche.

As we grew older, stories thrilled us, delighted us, entertained us, and sometimes even frightened the heck out of us. Who amongst us has not read a good novel and hung on every word as the villain or heroine teetered between life and death in some thrilling adventure? Stories move us; they tug at our emotions, heighten our awareness, provoke us to action, propel us into the future, or perhaps just take us back to a place where time was slower, and we felt relaxed and safe. Stories share knowledge, communicate life experiences like harrowing journeys, first loves and heartbreaking tragedies; stories have an emotional impact on our listener, and sometimes the impact lasts forever.

Interestingly enough, psychological and scientific research supports my anecdotal ramblings about the impact of well-told stories on the intellect and emotions of an audience. Research done by Uri Hasson, a neuroscientist at Princeton University, reveals that when we tell stories to individuals or an audience, we can actually transfer our experiences directly to their brains.[136] In other words, they empathize with us; they feel what we feel. Dr. Hasson has proven that when you tell an audience a story, you can actually get the audience's brains to synchronize with each other. In one study, Hasson told personal stories to five individuals while they were undergoing a magnetic resonance imaging (MRI) brain scan. Before the recorded story began, the five subjects' brains showed remarkably different activity; however, after they had listened to the story, their brains, according to Dr. Hasson, synchronized or became, as he refers to it, aligned.

Going a step further, Hasson had the five subjects listen to the stories played backwards and then nonsense sounds put together into words; then scrambled sentences. The subjects' brains showed some superficial synchronization during these exercises, but it was not until the full story was played that the subjects' brains became fully aligned. In another experiment,

Hasson had Russian speakers and English speakers listen to the exact same story told in their respective languages. Regardless of language, their brain activity still aligned. Joshua Gowin, Ph.D., writing in *Psychology Today*, reported this fascinating account of Dr. Hasson's experiments:

A team of scientists at Princeton, led by Uri Hasson, had a woman tell a story while in an MRI scanner. Functional MRI scans detect brain activity by monitoring blood flow; when a brain region is active it needs more blood to provide oxygen and nutrients. The active regions light up on a computer screen.

They recorded her story on a computer and monitored her brain activity as she spoke. She did this twice, once in English and once in Russian; she was fluent in both languages. They then had a group of volunteers listen to the stories through headphones while they had their brains scanned.

All of the volunteers spoke English, but none understood Russian. After the volunteers heard the story, Hasson asked them some questions to see how much of each story they understood. When the woman spoke English, the volunteers understood her story, and their brains synchronized. When she had activity in her insula, an emotional brain region, the listeners did too. When her frontal cortex lit up, so did theirs. By simply telling a story, the woman could plant ideas, thoughts, and emotions into the listeners' brains.

When you tell a story to a friend, you can transfer experiences directly to their brain. They feel what you feel. They empathize. What's more, when communicating most effectively, you can get a group of people's brains to synchronize their activity. As you relate someone's desires through a story, they become the desires of the audience. When trouble develops, they gasp in unison, and when desires are fulfilled they smile together.[137]

Stories have always been a part of human interaction both in premodern times when oral histories and family legends were passed from generation to generation, and later when the printing press made written publication possible. Likewise, stories have been a part of our business communications for as long as there has been commerce. Belly-to-belly salesmen, relying on their jovial nature and "gift of gab," have entertained customers with stories, and professionals have used stories to demonstrate their past successes in problem solving. But it has only been recently that the businesses community has grasped the real power of effective storytelling. Consider the innumerable television commercials that rely on short stories to communicate their message and sell a product. Whether it's Dick's Sporting Goods telling the poignant story of a kid growing from childhood into adolescence and then going off to college all around a basketball goal, or the story of the Budweiser Clydesdale horses who intervene in the "Best Buds" ad to bring a puppy back home, the stories are powerful tools in touching our emotions and invoking both nostalgia and memory.

Scientists tell us that storytelling evokes a strong neurological response. Neuroeconomist Paul Zak says it like this, "It is quiet and dark. The theater is hushed. James Bond skirts along the edge of a building as his enemy takes aim. Here in the audience, heart rates increase and palms sweat. I know this to be true because instead of enjoying the movie myself, I am measuring the brain activity of a dozen viewers. For me, excitement has a different source: I am watching an amazing neural ballet in which a story line changes the activity of people's brains."[138] Most businesspeople have now grasped informally what Zak has proven time and time again in his lab. Storytelling is a powerful tool that can be used for practical purposes in marketing, motivation, and other business endeavors. James Twitchell, a professor of English and advertising at the University of Florida, says that "we seem hardwired to emote when someone tells us a powerful story." Twitchell, an expert on branding and advertising goes on to say, "the only way to distinguish an interchangeable product is to tell a story about it, and the stories themselves become the repositories of value."[139] I believe Professor Twitchell has it right. Telling stories that convey to your audience that you have experience with the subject you are discussing will build confidence and trust and will distinguish you from others. Storytelling does at least three things for you.

- **Stories allow you to communicate in a casual way that can be easily understood**—A good story has a theme, a setting, a plot, characters, and a resolution. If you artfully craft your experiences into a story with these elements, your audience or listener will follow without getting hung up on details. Stories are often described similarly to dreams; they must be vivid and continuous.

- **Stories communicate depth**—You have lived it time and time again. You are, by implication, telling them that you have seen their specific issue or problem and you know the path to resolution.

- **A good story lets your reader or audience play a part**— They will be able to see themselves as a character in the thematic plot you are describing and, hopefully, visualize your role in their story's resolution. Stories build credibility and they invite questions that provide you an opportunity to deepen that credibility through more specific references to your listener's current situation.

On your journey to becoming Extraordinary, you cannot ignore the importance of stories and the impact they have on how people think and make decisions. If you learn to be a storyteller, you can influence people's opinions, you can change their opinions, and you can motivate them to follow you. Revive that old skill you had as a child, with an inexhaustible imagination, and rekindle your storytelling. Tell teaching stories, tell stories about danger, and tell inspirational stories. Tell stories about yourself. You might discover that you are pretty good at it.

## What makes a good story?

A good story, first and foremost, has a topic that is interesting to the listener and gets them emotionally involved. It must capture their attention early and allow them to see themselves in the story. This is particularly important when you are telling a story that is illustrative of a problem that you solved and you want your listener to associate themselves with the problem and the resolution.

I teach negotiations in a Mergers and Acquisitions Academy course in which I hope to let students live the difficulties and vagaries of negotiating with emotional sellers (of businesses). I tell the story of Theo Bean, the owner of a small business that had received a substantial offer for the purchase of his business. The buyer, let's call him Hans, was at lunch with Theo when he made the offer.

At one point, after the offer had been made, Theo looked at Hans and said, "Hans that is a very handsome watch you have on. I really like it." Hans held up his wrist, looked lovingly at the watch a moment too long, and said, "Thank you, Theo, it is a nice watch. It is a Patek Phillippe—my grandmother gave it to me years ago when I graduated from college." "Well, it is a handsome watch," Theo said.

Hans then brought the subject of the sale back to the conversation asking Theo what he thought of the offer price. Theo commented that he thought the price was fine and he was willing to do the deal. He then paused for what seemed like an eternity keeping his head down looking at his lunch plate. He finally looked up and said, "Hans, I'm happy to do the deal at your price…if you will throw in the watch." Hans was shocked and said with genuine amazement, "Theo, I can't throw in the watch; my grandmother, who passed away ten years ago gave me this watch." Theo looked Hans directly in the eyes, and unflinchingly, said, "NO DEAL!"

The point of this story is that when you are negotiating with emotional people, you must understand what is driving their emotional reactions. Theo didn't want the watch; he just didn't want the deal. But the real point is that this is a good story. My students are on the edge of their seats, if for only a minute or so, waiting to hear if Hans gave Theo the watch. It's a good story because it evokes the listener's emotions for the plight of the parties—Theo and his offer price, and Hans and his grandmother. They can sympathize with Hans, and they are just as shocked as Hans was when Theo so brazenly asked for the watch. They reflect on their own grandmothers and how they would have felt. In other words, they put themselves in the story.

In addition to interesting content, a good story has good form. It starts with a clear beginning, presents a conflict, proposes a resolution, and finishes with a definitive ending. This format is not new; it generally follows what is referred to as Freytag's Pyramid, named after a nineteenth century novelist, Gustav Freytag, who noticed patterns in the plots of stories and novels and built a diagram to help him analyze them.[140]

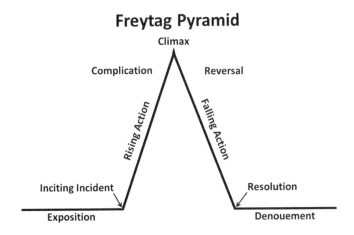

Most of the stories that you and I read as children, as well as most of the stuff we read today, generally follows Freytag's Pyramid. If you consider the stories of *The Three Little Pigs*, *Goldilocks and the Three Bears*, *Cinderella*, and a host of others, you will find the same formula; the beginning of the story, the conflict or complication that soon develops, the climax with some huffing and puffing, the reversal when we can see the end developing, and finally a resolution to the conflict. In fact, most of the simple stories that you and I tell when we are conveying events or activities to friends follow the pyramid. We set the situation up, build to the conflict or issue at hand, and then take our listeners to resolution.

On your journey to become Extraordinary, you have marvelous opportunities to tell stories. Don't let those stories happen randomly. Be proactive in finding opportunities to use stories to persuade others to see your point of view or to explain your position on issues. Use the Pyramid as a tool. You can be assured that your listener is programmed to hear the story in the Pyramid format. So capitalize on it.

Good stories follow a pattern, have interesting content, and are often laced with bits of tension and surprise to keep your listeners attentive and to give them that emotional high or low when they hear the end of the story. Learn to be a storyteller. It will make you a better listener and an inspirational leader. And, by the way, Theo never got the watch and he never did the deal.

## What makes a good storyteller?

A good storyteller is authentic, animated, authoritative, and at ease. The best storytellers are not necessarily the slickest orators, the most articulate speakers, and certainly not the most educated scholars. In fact, sometimes the best storytellers are the antithesis of these. A few years ago, Kimberly "Sweet Brown" Wilkins was the victim of an apartment fire and immediately after escaping the blaze, she was interviewed by a local television reporter. Here is what she said: "Well, I woke up to get me a cold pop and then I thought somebody was barbecuing. I said, 'Oh Lord Jesus, it's a fire.' Then I ran out, I didn't grab no shoes or nothin'. Jesus, I ran for my life. And then the smoke got me, I got bronchitis. Ain't nobody got time for that!"[141]

The interview went viral on YouTube and, as of the last time I checked, it has been viewed 12,264,339 times. Why is it so popular? The words are far from elegant, there are only 57 of them and they only last 41 seconds. The reason is, of course, Ms. Wilkins, in the moment, was a great storyteller. Her story had a beginning, as she described where she was and what she was doing when the fire began. It had a climax, as she escaped with no shoes. It had a resolution when she let us know she had escaped but got bronchitis. And, finally, the story had an ending with her near famous line, "Ain't nobody got time for that!" She was, in the moment, a great storyteller; her animation and excitement was palpable, she was authoritative and deliberate in describing her decision process, she was believable, and she seemed perfectly comfortable telling her story. Good storytellers possess these characteristics and can call on them at will.

I believe consistently good storytellers have three other things in common.

- **First, they are prepared**—They know what they want to say and they are sure of their facts. The result is a confidence that does not require fumbling for ideas; they come naturally because the storyteller is well prepared.

- **Second, good storytellers can paint a picture for the mind**—They give description and imagery that the listener can see, feel and smell. Moe Levine, one of the most celebrated trial lawyers in America once shocked a jury by painting a dramatic picture of his client. Here is what he said. "As you know, about an hour ago we broke for lunch. I saw the bailiff come and take you all as a group to have lunch in the jury room. Then I saw the defense attorney, Mr. Horowitz. He and his client decided to go to lunch together. The judge and court clerk went to lunch. So, I turned to my client, Harold, and said 'Why don't you and I go to lunch together?' We went across the street to that little restaurant and had lunch. (Significant pause.) Ladies and gentlemen, I just had lunch with my client. He has no arms. He has to eat like a dog. Thank you very much."[142]

  Levine painted a picture that the jury could not only see; they could feel it. They could imagine themselves in the client's condition. He reportedly won one of the largest settlements in the history of the state of New York.

- **Finally, good storytellers know how to "pull a rabbit out of the hat"**—They know how to surprise you when you least expect it. Believe it or not this is a learned skill. But it requires you to know your audience; where they are from, the culture they were raised in, their value systems and issues. The ancient Greeks had a word for it: "kairos," the right, critical or opportune moment.

Three years ago, I was having a fee discussion with a client, John, who was asking for a very large reduction in the billing for certain work that was yet to be performed. I decided to make a point by telling him a story from a personal experience that I knew he would not expect. Here is the true story that was not planned, but just happened when I decided to pull the "rabbit out of the hat" trick:

John, I used to own an Alfa Romeo Giulietta Spider and I needed to find a dual side draft Weber carburetor for the car. I went to a junkyard and asked the proprietor if he had the part I needed. He said of course, and took me over to a 50-gallon drum that was literally full of dual side draft Weber carburetors.

He handed me the part and I asked how much I owed him. He responded, without thinking, that the price was $50. I acted indignant and said, "Bob, you must be kidding. The carburetor is only worth $20 at most and you have a few hundred of them in this barrel." Bob said, "I would rather burn this carburetor up than sell it to you for less than I think its worth. You see, I know that you are going to tell everyone what you paid for it, and then they will expect me to sell it to them for $20."

Bob then picked up a can of gasoline that was sitting nearby and poured it over the carburetor. He then struck a match, set it on fire, and we watched it burn together until it turned black.

My client listened to my story and did not appear amused. All he said was, "Larry, I didn't know you felt that strongly about the billing for this work. Just be fair and bill me what you think it is worth." I breathed a sigh of relief, and gently put the rabbit back in the hat. I don't recommend this tactic for all situations since it does carry more than a modicum of risk. However, if you know your audience and you are prepared, you can make it work for you.

## Tell your own story

While we all love a good story, the best stories are the ones that you have lived, are a testament to your experiences, and you can use to add depth and color to your already overboard preparation. Whether you are about to perform brain surgery, build a house, play third base for your office softball team, or advise a client on a course of action, the people you encounter all want to know one thing. Have you ever done this before, or is this your first rodeo, cowboy? Preparation and a crisp presentation will help, but there is no substitute for being able to tell stories about your experiences and how you solved problems just like the one they might be discussing with you at the moment. So embrace your own story and be prepared to tell it. Let me conclude with a few suggestions that might help.

- **Write your story down**—Start with your childhood and create a story that recounts who you are and where you came from. Make it honest and factual and let it build over time into what you are today. I just recently asked an old high-school friend if he had ever played golf at the East Lake Golf course where the Tournament of Champions is held each year in Atlanta. He said no, and reminded me, unashamedly, that he came from the "projects" in middle Georgia. Similarly, I had a colleague, who graduated number one in his Emory University business school class, who almost rejoices at the opportunity to tell any group of people that his grandparents had once been sharecroppers in Alabama. In these examples, these guys have a story to tell and they are not afraid to tell it. The act of putting your story into words will be cathartic and will frame your story for future telling. Additionally, it will provide a written legacy of your life that tells your story long after you are gone.

- **Create a pithy summary of your story**—Once you have your story on paper or on your hard drive, summarize it into crisp bullet points that you can remember easily. Then practice telling your story to the mirror in the privacy of your home. Look for those pivotal moments that impacted your life and created your personality and belief systems. Relish the sweet memories of those perfect days when time just lingered and you were the happiest. Reflect on the harsh memories that you can't forget; they are a part of who you are. I love to begin a conversation with someone I do not know by asking them directly to "tell me your story." I listen intently looking for clues that will tell me who they really are, and then I get prepared for the reciprocal question of "what's your story?"

- **Remember one more thing**—It's a sorry dog who won't wag his own tail. Thank You, Little Richard.

Your journey to Extraordinary will be both exciting and treacherous, filled with magnificent successes and miserable failures. Regardless of your calling—business, education, medicine, law, engineering, music or the arts—your travels will craft a unique story that only you can tell. Embrace the journey and boldly tell your story. Chances are you will find an audience all too willing to listen.

I began, fellow-traveler, by saying that this is my story, but I want it to become yours. It's in your hands now. Travel well.

# Appendix I
# Puzzles and Solutions

## Puzzle Number 1

A man is on his way home when he meets another man in a mask. He immediately turns around and runs the other way. What is the situation?

### Solution

*There is a baseball game; the man is on his way to home plate running from third base when he meets the catcher in his face mask. He immediately turns around and heads back to third base.*

## Puzzle Number 2

A man pushed his car. He stopped when he reached a hotel at which point he knew he was bankrupt. Why?

### Solution

*The man pushing the car was a player in a monopoly game and his game piece was a car.*

## Puzzle Number 3

A man walks into a bar and asks the barman for a glass of water. The barman pulls out a gun and points it at the man. The man says "Thank you" and walks out.

### Solution

*The man who walks into the bar has hiccups. The bartender recognizes the problem and pulls a gun to scare the hiccups away. The home remedy works and the man thanks the bartender.*

271

# Appendix II
# Questionnaire

## Are you a night owl or an early bird?

Our bodies have an internal clock, called the circadian rhythm, that tells us when it is the best time for us to sleep, wake up, eat, exercise, learn and a number of other things. Not everyone's body clock is the same. Some people feel their best in the morning, while other people feel their best at night. Some people can go to sleep easily early in the evening, while other people have trouble going to sleep before midnight. Understanding your body clock will help you to understand what times of the day you are more productive and what times are the best for you to sleep.

## Instructions

A. Read each question carefully.
B. Answer each question as honestly as possible.
   Do not go back and check your answers.
   Your first response is usually the most accurate.
C. Answer ALL questions.

## Questionnaire

1. **What time would you get up if you were entirely free to plan your day?**

| Time | Score (please circle) |
| --- | --- |
| 5:00 — 6:29 a.m. | 5 |
| 6:30 — 7:44 a.m. | 4 |
| 7:45 — 9:44 a.m. | 3 |
| 9:45 — 10:59 a.m. | 2 |
| 11:00 — 11:59 a.m. | 1 |
| Midday — 5:00 a.m. | 0 |

2. **What time would you go to bed if you were entirely free to plan your evening?**

| Time | Score (please circle) |
| --- | --- |
| 8:00 — 8:59 p.m. | 5 |
| 9:00 — 10:14 p.m. | 4 |
| 10:15 p.m. — 12:29 a.m. | 3 |
| 12:30 — 1:44 a.m. | 2 |
| 1:45 — 2:59 a.m. | 1 |
| 3:00 a.m. — 8:00 p.m. | 0 |

3. **If there is a specific time at which you have to get up in the morning, to what extent do you depend on being woken up by an alarm clock?**

|  | Score (please circle) |
|---|:---:|
| Not at all dependent | 4 |
| Slightly dependent | 3 |
| Fairly dependent | 2 |
| Very dependent | 1 |

4. **How easy do you find it to get up in the morning (when you are not woken up unexpectedly)?**

|  | Score (please circle) |
|---|:---:|
| Not at all easy | 1 |
| Not very easy | 2 |
| Fairly easy | 3 |
| Very easy | 4 |

5. How alert do you feel during the first half-hour after you wake up in the morning?

|  | Score (please circle) |
|---|---|
| Not at all alert | 1 |
| Slightly alert | 2 |
| Fairly alert | 3 |
| Very alert | 4 |

6. How hungry do you feel during the first half-hour after you wake up in the morning?

|  | Score (please circle) |
|---|---|
| Not at all hungry | 1 |
| Slightly hungry | 2 |
| Fairly hungry | 3 |
| Very hungry | 4 |

7. **During the first half-hour after you wake up in the morning, how tired do you feel?**

|  | **Score** (please circle) |
|---|---|
| Very tired | 1 |
| Fairly tired | 2 |
| Fairly refreshed | 3 |
| Very refreshed | 4 |

8. **If you have no commitment the next day, what time would you go to bed compared to your usual bedtime?**

|  | **Score** (please circle) |
|---|---|
| Seldom or never later | 4 |
| Less than one hour later | 3 |
| 1-2 hours later | 2 |
| More than two hours later | 1 |

9. You have decided to engage in some physical exercise. A friend suggests that you do this for one hour twice a week and the best time for him/her is between 7:00 – 8:00 a.m. Bearing in mind nothing but your own internal "clock," how do you think you would perform?

|  | Score<br>(please circle) |
| --- | --- |
| Would be in good form | 4 |
| Would be in reasonable form | 3 |
| Would find it difficult | 2 |
| Would find it very difficult | 1 |

10. At what time of day do you feel you become tired as a result of need for sleep?

| Time | Score<br>(please circle) |
| --- | --- |
| 8:00 – 8:59 p.m. | 5 |
| 9:00 – 10:14 p.m. | 4 |
| 10:15 p.m. – 12:44 a.m. | 3 |
| 12:45 – 1:59 a.m. | 2 |
| 2:00 – 3:00 a.m. | 1 |

11. **You want to be at your peak performance for a test that you know is going to be mentally exhausting and will last for two hours. You are entirely free to plan your day. Considering only your own internal "clock," which ONE of the four testing times would you choose?**

| Time | Score (please circle) |
|---|---|
| 8:00 — 10:00 a.m. | 4 |
| 11:00 a.m. — 1:00 p.m. | 3 |
| 3:00 — 5:00 p.m. | 2 |
| 7:00 — 9:00 p.m. | 1 |

12. **If you got into bed at 11:00 p.m., how tired would you be?**

| | Score (please circle) |
|---|---|
| Not at all tired | 1 |
| A little tired | 2 |
| Fairly tired | 3 |
| Very tired | 4 |

13. For some reason, you have gone to bed several hours later than usual, but there is no need to get up at any particular time the next morning. Which ONE of the following are you most likely to do?

**Score**
(please circle)

| | |
|---|---|
| Will wake up at usual time, but will NOT fall back asleep | 4 |
| Will wake up at usual time and will doze thereafter | 3 |
| Will wake up at usual time but will fall asleep again | 2 |
| Will not wake up until later than usual | 1 |

14. One night you have to remain awake between 4:00 – 6:00 a.m. in order to carry out a night watch. You have no commitments the next day. Which ONE of the alternatives will suit you best?

**Score**
(please circle)

| | |
|---|---|
| Would not go to bed until watch was over | 1 |
| Would take a nap before and sleep after | 2 |
| Would take a good sleep before and nap after | 3 |
| Would sleep only before watch | 4 |

15. **You have to do two hours of hard physical work. You are entirely free to plan your day and considering only your own internal "clock," which ONE of the following times would you choose?**

| Time | Score (please circle) |
|---|---|
| 8:00 − 10:00 a.m. | 4 |
| 11:00 a.m.− 1:00 p.m. | 3 |
| 3:00 − 5:00 p.m. | 2 |
| 7:00 − 9:00 p.m. | 1 |

16. **You have decided to engage in hard physical exercise. A friend suggests that you do this together for one hour twice a week and the best time for him/her is between 10:00 − 11:00 p.m. Bearing in mind nothing else but your own internal "clock," how well do you think you would perform?**

| | Score (please circle) |
|---|---|
| Would be in good form | 4 |
| Would be in reasonable form | 3 |
| Would find it difficult | 2 |
| Would find it very difficult | 1 |

17. **Suppose that you can choose your school hours. Assume that you went to school for five hours per day and that school was interesting and enjoyable. Which five consecutive hours would you select?**

| Time | Score (please circle) |
|---|---|
| 5 hrs starting between 4 a.m. – 7:59 a.m. | 5 |
| 5 hrs starting between 8 a.m. – 8:59 a.m. | 4 |
| 5 hrs starting between 9 a.m. – 1:59 p.m. | 3 |
| 5 hrs starting between 2 p.m. – 4:59 p.m. | 2 |
| 5 hrs starting between 5 p.m. – 3:59 a.m. | 1 |

18. **At what time of the day do you think that you reach your "feeling best" peak?**

| Time | Score (please circle) |
|---|---|
| 5:00 – 7:59 a.m. | 5 |
| 8:00 – 9:59 a.m. | 4 |
| 10:00 a.m.– 4:59 p.m. | 3 |
| 5:00 – 9:59 p.m. | 2 |
| 10:00 p.m.– 4:59 a.m. | 1 |

19. **One hears about "morning" and "evening" types of people. Which ONE of these types do you consider yourself to be?**

**Score**
(please circle)

| | |
|---|---|
| Definitely a "morning" type | 6 |
| More a "morning" type than an "evening" type | 4 |
| More an "evening" type than a "morning" type | 2 |
| Definitely an "evening" type | 0 |

This questionnaire has 19 questions, each with a number of points. First, add up the points you circled and enter your total morningness-eveningness score here:

Scores can range from 16-86. Scores of 41 and below indicate "evening types." Scores of 59 and above indicate "morning types." Scores between 42-58 indicate "intermediate types."[143]

# Notes

1. Gary Martin, "The meaning and origin of the expression: Curiosity killed the cat," The Phrase Finder, https://www.phrases.org.uk/meanings/curiosity-killed-the-cat.html (accessed on March 17, 2018).

2. Todd Kashdan, *Curious?* (New York: William Morrow, 2009).

3. George Loewenstein, "The Psychology of Curiosity: A Review and Reinterpretation," *Semantics Scholar American Psychological Association,* 1994, Vol. 116, No.1, 75-98.

4. *Ibid.*

5. Hans Blumenberg, *The Legitimacy of the Modern Age,* trans. Robert M. Wallace (Cambridge: MIT Press, 1986).

6. Loewenstein, "The Psychology of Curiosity", 75-98.

7. Alan Shepard, Deke Slayton, Jay Barbree and Howard Benedict, *Moon Shot: The Inside Story of America's Race to the Moon* (Nashville: Turner Publishing, 1994).

8. Kathryn Zickuhr and Lee Rainie, "A Snapshot of Reading in America," Pew Research Center, January 16, 2014, http://www.pewinternet.org/2014/01/16/a-snapshot-of-reading-in-america.

9. Jordan Weissmann, "The Decline of the American Book Lover," *The Atlantic*, January 21, 2014.

10. Bijan Stephen, "You Won't Believe How Little Americans Read," *Time*, June 22, 2014.

11. Andrew Perrin, "Book Reading 2016," Pew Research Center, September 1, 2016, http://www.pewinternet.org/2016/09/01/book-reading-2016/.

12. Harry Shearer, *The Simpsons Movie*, DVD. Directed by David Silverman. Los Angeles: Twentieth Century Fox, 2007.

13. Steve Siebold, *How Rich People Think* (Naperville: Simple Truths, 2014).

14. Thomas Jefferson, Abigail Adams, and John Adams, *The Adams-Jefferson Letters: The Complete Correspondence between Thomas Jefferson and Abigail and John Adams*, ed. Lester J. Cappon (Chapel Hill: University of North Carolina Press, 1988).

15. Shannon Selin, "Bonaparte the Bookworm—Napoleon was an avid reader; so what were his favourite books?" Military History Now, April 15, 2015, http://militaryhistorynow.com/2015/04/15/bonaparte.

16. Harriet Rubin, "C.E.O. Libraries Reveal Keys to Success," *New York Times*, July 21, 2007.

17. Marguerite Ward, "Warren Buffet's reading routine could make you smarter, science suggests," CNBC, November 16, 2016, https://www.cnbc.com/2016/11/16/warren-buffetts-reading-routine-could-make-you-smarter-suggests-science.html.

18. Richard Feloni, "Twenty Books Mark Zuckerberg Thinks Everyone Should Read," Business Insider, October 22, 2015, http://www.businessin-

sider.com/mark-zuckerberg-book-recommendations-2015-10.

19. Tom Corley, *Rich Habits: The Daily Success Habits of Wealthy Individuals* (Minneapolis: Langdon Street Press, 2010).

20. Sigmund Freud, "Quotable Quote," GoodReads, https://www.goodreads.com/quotes/332208 (accessed March 17, 2018).

21. Ron Livingston, Office Space, DVD. Directed by Mike Judge. Los Angeles: Twentieth Century Fox, 1999.

22. Robert Frost, *The Poetry of Robert Frost*, ed. Edward Connery Lathem (New York: Henry Holt and Co., 1979).

23. Teresa Amabile, Constance Noonan Hadley, and Steven J. Kramer, "Creativity Under the Gun," Harvard Business Review, August, 2002.

24. John Fitzherbert, *The Book of Husbandry* (Columbia: Andesite Press, 2015).

25. Takeo Watanabe, Y. Yotsumoto, LH Chang, R. Ni, R. Pierce, G.J. Andersen, Y. Sasaki, "White Matter in the Older Brain is More Plastic Than in the Younger Brain," Nature Communications, November 19, 2014, https://www.ncbi.nlm.nih.gov/pubmed/25407566.

26. Mario D. Garrett, "Brain Plasticity in Older Adults: Learning new tricks in older age," Psychology Today, April 27, 2013.

27. Karl Duncker, *A Qualitative (Experimental and Theoretical) Study of Productive Thinking (Solving of Comprehensible problems)* (Worcester, Mass: Clark University, 1926).

28. *Ibid.*

29. Paul Sloane, *Lateral Thinking Puzzlers* (New York: Puzzle Wright Press, 2016).

30. Ben Waber, Jennifer Magnolfi and Greg Lindsay, "Workspaces

That Move People," *Harvard Business Review*, October 2014.

31. Nielsen, "Why Collaboration Leads to Higher-Impact Innovations," Nielsen Report, December 01, 2015, http://www.nielsen.com/us/en/insights/news/2015/why-collaboration-leads-to-higher-impact-innovations.html.

32. Adam Smith, *The Wealth of Nations* (London: W. Strahan and T. Cadell, 1776).

33. Russell Crowe, *A Beautiful Mind*, DVD. Directed by Ron Howard. Universal City: Universal Pictures, 2001.

34. Friedrich Nietzsche, *Human, All-Too-Human: Parts One and Two* (New York: Dover Publications, 2006).

35. Irving L. Janis, *Victims of Groupthink: A psychological study of foreign-policy decisions and fiascoes* (New York: Houghton Mifflin, 1972).

36. Slim B. Sitkin, *Learning Through Failure: The Strategy of Small Losses* (Austin: University of Texas, 1990).

37. Jack V. Matson, *The art of innovation: Using intelligent fast failure* (University Park: Pennsylvania State University, 1991).

38. Butch Rigby, "History Laugh-O-Gram," Thank You Walt Disney, Inc., https://thankyouwaltdisney.org/history/ (accessed March 17, 2018).

39. Rachel Hodin, "35 Famous People Who Were Painfully Rejected Before Making It Big," Thought Catalog, October 14, 2013, https://thoughtcatalog.com/rachel-hodin/2013/10/35-famous-people-who-were-painfully-rejected-before-making-it-big/.

40. Henry Petroski, *To Engineer is Human: The Role of Failure in Successful Design* (New York: Vintage Publications, 1992).

41. Tanza Loudenback, "Spanx founder Sara Blakely learned an

important lesson about failure from her dad—now she's passing it on to her 4 kids," Business Insider, October 14, 2016, http://www.businessinsider.com/spanx-founder-sara-blakely-redefine-failure-2016-10.

42. Kevin Daum, "37 Quotes from Thomas Edison that will Inspire Success," Inc., February 11, 2016.

43. Thomas Howell, "New Sonnets and Pretty Pamphlets," Historically Speaking, January 19, 2011, https://idiomation.wordpress.com/tag/new-sonnets-and-pretty-pamphlets/.

44. Samuel Butler, *Hudibras* (New York: CreateSpace Independent Publishing, 2017).

45. Clint Eastwood, *Dirty Harry*, DVD. Directed by Don Siegel. Hollywood: Warner Brothers, 1971.

46. Steven Pressfield, *Do the Work* (New York: Black Irish Books, 2015).

47. Ozgun Atasoy, "Your Thoughts Can Release Abilities Beyond Normal Limits," *Scientific American*, August 13, 2013.

48. *Ibid.*

49. Walt Disney, "Quotable Quote," GoodReads, https://www.goodreads.com/quotes/1367382 (accessed March 16, 2018).

50. Carmine Gallo, "Steve Jobs' Advice: "Dream Bigger," *Forbes*, December 14, 2010.

51. Emely de Vet, Rob M.A. Nelissen, Marcel Zeelenberg and Denise de Ridder, "Ain't no mountain high enough? Setting high weight loss goals predict effort and short-term weight loss," Journal of Health Psychology 18, no. 5 (August 29, 2012): 638-647.

52. Napoleon Hill, *Think and Grow Rich* (Pennsylvania: Sound Wisdom, 2016).

53. John Naughton, "Steve Jobs: Stanford commencement address, June 2005," The Guardian, October 8, 2011, https://www.theguardian.com/technology/2011/oct/09/steve-jobs-stanford-commencement-address.

54. Alexander Pope, "An Essay on Criticism," Poetry Foundation, October 13, 2009, https://www.poetryfoundation.org/articles/69379.

55. Glen Stansberry, "How to Become a Modern Day Renaissance Man (or Woman)," Gentlemint, April 14, 2017, http://blog.gentlemint.com/2017/jan/18/renaissance-man/.

56. Robin Williams, *Dead Poets Society*, DVD. Directed by Peter Weir. Burbank: Touchstone Pictures, 1989.

57. Edwin Rolfe and Lester Fuller, *Murder in the Glass Room* (New York: Bantam Books, 1948).

58. Jim Collins, *Good to Great: Why Some Companies Make the Leap... and Others Don't* (New York: Harper Business, 2011).

59. Diane Coutu, "How Resilience Works," Harvard Business Review, May 2002.

60. *Ibid.*

61. John Capgrave, *The Life of Saint Katherine* (Kalamazoo: Medieval Institute Publications, 1999).

62. Hugh Rhodes, *The Boke of Nurture for Men Servants and Children* (Charleston: Nabu Press, 2012).

63. Ecclesiastes 9:4 KJV

64. Zawn Villines, "The Psychology of Risk-Taking," Good Therapy.org, May 7, 2013, https://www.goodtherapy.org/blog/risks-adrenaline-benefits-neuroticism-0418137.

65. *Ibid.*

66. Bill Treasurer, *Courage Goes to Work: How to Build Backbones, Boost Performance, and Get Results* (Oakland: Berrett-Koehler Publishers, 2008).

67. Hill, *Think and Grow Rich.*

68. Stuart Diamond. *Getting More: How to Negotiate to Achieve Your Goals in the Real World.* New York: Crown Publishing, 2009.

69. Linda Sapadin, *Master Your Fears: How to Triumph Over Your Worries and Get on with Your Life* (Hoboken: John Wiley & Sons, 2004).

70. *Ibid.*

71. *Ibid.*

72. Hodin, "35 Famous People."

73. Christian B. Keller and Ethan S. Rafuse, "The Civil War Battlefield Staff Ride in the Twenty-first Century," *Civil War History* 62, no.2 (June 2016): 201.

74. Dan Favale, "Michael Jordan's Unofficial Guide to Success in the NBA," The Bleacher Report, February 14, 2013, http://bleacherreport.com/articles/1529861.

75. Liz Funk, "The Hidden Power in Trusting Your Gut Instincts," Fast Company, April 7, 2016, https://www.fastcompany.com/3058609.

76. Rachel Gillett, "How Walt Disney, Oprah Winfrey, and 19 Other Successful People Rebounded After Getting Fired," Business Insider, October 7, 2015, https://www.inc.com/business-insider/21-successful-people-who-rebounded-after-getting-fired.html.

77. Winston Churchill Quotes. BrainyQuote.com, Xplore Inc, 2018.

https://www.brainyquote.com/authors/winston_churchill, accessed March 19, 2018.

78. Robert Greene, *The 33 Strategies of War* (London: Penguin Books, 2006).

79. Clint Eastwood, *Magnum Force*, DVD. Directed by Ted Post. Hollywood: Warner Brothers, 1973.

80. Elena Holodny, "Everyone forgets the most important thing about the 1987 Black Monday stock market crash," Business Insider, October 19, 2017, http://www.businessinsider.com/1987-black-monday-stock-market-crash-most-important-lesson-2017-10.

81. John Ray, *A Complete Collection of English Proverbs* (London: Forgotten Books, 2017).

82. *Ibid.*

83. Justin Fox, "Instinct Can Beat Analytical Thinking," Harvard Business Review, June 20, 2014.

84. Gerd Gigerenzer, Peter M. Todd and the ABC Research Group, Simple Heuristics That Make Us Smart (Oxford: Oxford University Press, 2000).

85. Malcolm Gladwell, *Blink: The Power of Thinking without Thinking* (New York: Little, Brown and Company, 2007).

86. Timothy D. Wilson, *Strangers to Ourselves: Discovering the Adaptive Unconscious* (Cambridge: Belknap Press, 2004).

87. Rita McGrath, "Transient Advantage," *Harvard Business Review*, June 2013.

88. Philip Gooden, *Skyscapers Hemlines and the Eddie Murphy Rule:*

*Life's Hidden Laws Rules & Theories* (New York: Bloomsbury Publishing, 2015).

89. Tim Hindle, *The Economist Guide to Management Ideas and Gurus* (New York: Bloomberg Press, 2008).

90. *Ibid.*

91. Nick Tasler, "Make Good Decisions Faster," *Harvard Business Review,* July 05, 2013.

92. Mark L. Feldman, Michael F. Spratt, and Michael Frederick Spratt, *Five Frogs on a Log, a Field Guide to Accelerated Transition in Mergers and Acquisitions* (New York: Harper Collins Publishers, 1998).

93. Eric Chester, *Reviving Work Ethic: A Leader's Guide to Ending Entitlement and Restoring Pride in the Emerging Workforce* (Austin: Greenleaf Book Group Press, 2012).

94. D'Vera Cohn, "Millennials—Confident, Connected, Open to Change," Pew Research Center, February 24, 2010, http://www.pewsocialtrends.org/2010/02/24/millennials-confident-connected-open-to-change/.

95. *Ibid.*

96. Chester, *Reviving Work Ethic.*

97. Alan B. Shepard and Deke Slayton, *Moon Shot: The Inside Story of America's Race to the Moon* (Nashville: Turner Publishing Incorporated, 1994).

98. Rachel Gillett, "5 Reasons Google is the Best Place to Work in America and No Other Company Can Touch it," Business Insider, April 28, 2016, http://www.businessinsider.com/google-is-the-best-company-to-work-for-in-america-2016-4.

99. Benjamin Looper, "Who is Southeast Restoration?" Southeast Restoration, 2017, https://southeastrestoration.com/about-us/.

100. Idalia Hill, "PwC Commits $320 Million to Help Improve Technology & Financial Capability of More Than 10 Million Students," PwC, New York, March 30, 2017, https://www.pwc.com/us/en/press-releases/2017/access-your-potential-aims-to-help-10-million-students.html.

101. Jacquelyn Smith, "The Insane Work Ethic of Mark Cuban, Jeff Bezos, and 14 Other Powerful Leaders," Business Insider, April 8, 2016, https://www.inc.com/business-insider/work-ethic-of-super-successful-people.html.

102. *Ibid.*

103. John Ray, "The Early Bird Catches the Worm," Historically Speaking, May 11, 2010, https://idiomation.wordpress.com/2010/05/11/the-early-bird-catches-the-worm/.

104. *Ibid.*

105. Steve Blank, "Here's why the First-Mover Advantage is Extremely Overrated," Business Insider, October 19, 2010, http://www.businessinsider.com/steve-blank-first-mover-advantage-overrated-2010-10.

106. Chaz Green, "The History of Search Engines & Google Domination," Kazooky Media, June 22, 2015, http://www.kazooky.com/the-history-of-search-engines-google-domination/.

107. Devon Glenn, "The History of Social Media from 1978-2012," AdWeek, February 16, 2012, http://www.adweek.com/digital/the-history-of-social-media-from-1978-2012-infographic/.

108. Sean Cooper, "Whatever happened to Netscape?" Engadget, May

10, 2014, https://www.engadget.com/2014/05/10/history-of-netscape/.

109. Brad Reed, "A Palm Technology Timeline," PC World, April 30, 2010, https://www.pcworld.com/article/195350.

110. Gerard J. Tellis & Peter N. Golder, Will and Vision: *How Latecomers Grow to Dominate Markets* (New York: McGraw-Hill, 2001).

111. *Ibid.*

112. Judith Orloff, *Emotional Freedom: Liberate Yourself from Negative Emotions and Transform Your Life* (New York: Harmony Books, 2009).

113. *Ibid.*

114. Kelly McGonigal, *The Willpower Instinct* (London: The Penguin Group, 2012).

115. Maria Konnikova, "The Struggles of a Psychologist Studying Self-Control," *The New Yorker*, October 9, 2014.

116. *Ibid.*

117. Orloff, *Emotional Freedom*, page.

118. Sarah Schnitker, "An Examination of Patience and Well-being," The Journal of Positive Psychology 7, no. 4 (June 26, 2012): 263-280.

119. *Ibid.*

120. Ken Harmon, "What Makes You Happy?" (speech, Kennesaw, GA, 2015).

121. Kira M. Newman, "Four Reasons to Cultivate Patience," Greater Good, April 4, 2016, https://greatergood.berkeley.edu/article/item/four_reasons_to_cultivate_patience.

122. Roger Dobson, "If You Want to Get Ahead, Be a Night Owl," Independent, March 24, 2013, https://www.independent.co.uk/life-style/

health-and-families/health-news/if-you-want-to-get-ahead-be-a-night-owl-8547115.html.

123. Rachel Sugar, "15 People Who Prove You Don't Have to Wake up Early to be Successful," Business Insider, July 12, 2015, http://www.businessinsider.com/successful-people-who-wake-up-late-2015-7.

124. Adam Hadhazy, "Life's Extremes: Early Birds vs. Night Owls," Live Science, October 2, 2011, https://www.livescience.com/16334-night-owls-early-birds-sleep-cycles.html.

125. Eric Jaffe, "Morning People vs. Night Owls: 9 Insights Backed by Science," Fast Company, May 19, 2015, https://www.fastcodesign.com/3046391.

126. Satoshi Kanazawa, "Why Night Owls Are More Intelligent Than Morning Larks," Psychology Today, May 9, 2010.

127. Michael Douglas, Wall Street, DVD. Directed by Oliver Stone. Los Angeles: Twentieth Century Fox, 1987.

128. Hill, Think and Grow Rich.

129. Arthur C. Brooks, "Abundance without Attachment," New York Times, December 12, 2014.

130. Ibid.

131. Curt Sampson, A Vision, Not a Blueprint—Weldon Wyatt and Sage Valley (Curt Sampson, 2007).

132. Charles Dickens, A Christmas Carol (London: Chapman & Hall, 1843).

133. Henry David Thoreau Quotes, BrainyQuote.com, Xplore Inc, https://www.brainyquote.com/authors/henry_david_thoreau (accessed March 15, 2018).

134. Ted Turner Quotes, BrainyQuote.com, Xplore Inc, https://www.brainyquote.com/authors/ted_turner (accessed March 15, 2018).

135. Little Richard Penniman, *Poor Dog* (California: Columbia Studios, 1966).

136. Uri Hasson, "This is your brain on communication," TED Talk, 14:52, February 18, 2016, https://www.ted.com/talks/uri_hasson_this_is_your_brain_on_communication.

137. Joshua Gowin, "Why Sharing Stories Brings People Together," *Psychology Today*, June 6, 2011.

138. Paul J. Zak, "Why Your Brain Loves Good Storytelling," *Harvard Business Review*, October 28, 2014.

139. James B. Twitchell, *Branded Nation: The Marketing of Megachurch, College Inc., and Museumworld* (New York: Simon & Schuster, 2004).

140. Gustav Freytag, *Freytag's Technique of the Drama: an exposition of dramatic composition and art*, trans. Elias J. MacEwan (Chicago: Scott, Foresman and Company, 1900), 115.

141. Kimberly Wilkins, "Ain't Nobody Got Time for That," YouTube Video, 0:41, October 28, 2012, https://www.youtube.com/watch?v=zGx-wbhkDjZM.

142. Moe Levine, "The Whole Man," Trebidi Tales, June 2016, https://tribeditales.wordpress.com/2016/06/19/whole-man-theory.

143. JA Horne and O. Ostberg, "A self -assessment questionnaire to determine morningness-eveningness in human circadian rhythms," *International Journal of Chronobiology*, no. 4 (1976): 97-100.

# Bibliography

Amabile, Teresa, Constance Noonan Hadley, and Steven J. Kramer. "Creativity Under the Gun." *Harvard Business Review*, August 1, 2002.

Atasoy, Ozgun. "Your Thoughts Can Release Abilities Beyond Normal Limits." *Scientific American*, August 13, 2013.

Blank, Steve. "Here's why the First-Mover Advantage is Extremely Overrated." Business Insider, October 19, 2010, http://www.businessinsider.com/steve-blank-first-mover-advantage-overrated-2010-10

Blumenberg, Hans. *The Legitimacy of the Modern Age*. trans. Robert M. Wallace. Cambridge: MIT Press, 1986.

Brooks, Arthur C. "Abundance without Attachment." *New York Times*, December 12, 2014.

Butler, Samuel. *Hudibras*. New York: CreateSpace Independent Publishing, 2017.

Capgrave, John. *The Life of Saint Katherine*. Kalamazoo: Medieval Institute Publications, 1999.

Chester, Eric. *Reviving Work Ethic: A Leader's Guide to Ending Entitlement and Restoring Pride in the Emerging Workforce*. Austin: Greenleaf Book Group Press, 2012.

Cohn, D'Vera. "Millennials – Confident, Connected, Open to Change." Pew Research Center, February 24, 2010, http://www.pewsocialtrends.org/2010/02/24/millennials-confident-connected-open-to-change/

Collins, Jim. *Good to Great: Why Some Companies Make the Leap... and Others Don't.* New York: Harper Business, 2011.

Cooper, Sean. "Whatever happened to Netscape?" Engadget, May 10, 2014, https://www.engadget.com/2014/05/10/history-of-netscape/

Corley, Tom. *Rich Habits: The Daily Success Habits of Wealthy Individuals.* (Minneapolis: Langdon Street Press, 2010).

Coutu, Diane. "How Resilience Works." Harvard Business Review, May 2002.

Crowe, Russell. *A Beautiful Mind*, DVD. Directed by Ron Howard. Universal City: Universal Pictures, 2001.

Daum, Kevin. "37 Quotes from Thomas Edison that will Inspire Success." Inc., February 11, 2016.

De Vet, Emely, Rob M.A. Nelissen, Marcel Zeelenberg and Denise de Ridder. "Ain't no mountain high enough? Setting high weight loss goals predict effort and short-term weight loss." *Journal of Health Psychology* 18, no. 5 (August 29, 2012): 638-647.

Diamond, Stuart, *Getting More: How to Negotiate to Achieve Your Goals in the Real World*, (New York: Crown Publishing, 2009).

Dickens, Charles. *A Christmas Carol.* London: Chapman & Hall, 1843.

Disney, Walt. "Quotable Quote." GoodReads. https://www.goodreads.com/quotes/1367382-all-our-dreams-can-come-true-if-we-have-the (accessed March 16, 2018).

Dobson, Roger. "If You Want to Get Ahead, Be a Night Owl." Independent, March 24, 2013. https://www.independent.co.uk/life-style/health-and-families/health-news/if-you-want-to-get-ahead-be-a-night-owl-8547115.html

Douglas, Michael. *Wall Street*. DVD. Directed by Oliver Stone. Los Angeles: Twentieth Century Fox, 1987.

Duncker, Karl. *A Qualitative (Experimental and Theoretical) Study of Productive Thinking (Solving of Comprehensible problems)*. Worcester, Mass: Clark University, 1926.

Eastwood, Clint. *Dirty Harry*, DVD. Directed by Don Siegel. Hollywood: Warner Brothers, 1971.

Eastwood, Clint. *Magnum Force*. DVD. Directed by Ted Post. Hollywood: Warner Brothers, 1973.

Favale, Dan. "Michael Jordan's Unofficial Guide to Success in the NBA." The Bleacher Report, February 14, 2013, http://bleacherreport.com/articles/1529861-michael-jordans-unofficial-guide-to-success-in-the-nba

Feldman, Michael F. Spratt, and Michael Frederick Spratt. *Five Frogs on a Log, a Field Guide to Accelerated Transition in Mergers and Acquisitions*. New York: Harper Collins Publishers, 1998.

Feloni, Richard. "Twenty Books Mark Zuckerberg Thinks Everyone Should Read." Business Insider, October 22, 2015, http://www.businessinsider.com/mark-zuckerberg-book-recommendations-2015-10

Fitzherbert, John. *The Book of Husbandry*. Columbia: Andesite Press, 2015.

Fox, Justin. "Instinct Can Beat Analytical Thinking." Harvard Business Review, June 20, 2014.

Freytag, Gustav. *Freytag's Technique of the Drama: an exposition of dramatic composition and art.* Translated by Elias J. MacEwan Chicago: Scott, Foresman and Company, 1900.

Frost, Robert. *The Poetry of Robert Frost*, ed. Edward Connery Lathem. New York: Henry Holt and Co., 1979.

Funk, Liz. "The Hidden Power in Trusting Your Gut Instincts." Fast Company, April 7, 2016, https://www.fastcompany.com/3058609/the-hidden-power-in-trusting-your-gut-instincts

Gallo, Carmine. "Steve Jobs' Advice: "Dream Bigger." *Forbes*, December 14, 2010.

Garrett, Mario D. "Brain Plasticity in Older Adults: Learning new tricks in older age." *Psychology Today*, April 27, 2013.

Gigerenzer, Gerd, Peter M. Todd and the ABC Research Group. *Simple Heuristics That Make Us Smart.* Oxford: Oxford University Press, 2000.

Gillett, Rachel. "5 Reasons Google is the Best Place to Work in America and No Other Company Can Touch it." Business Insider, April 28, 2016, http://www.businessinsider.com/google-is-the-best-company-to-work-for-in-america-2016-4

Gillett, Rachel. "How Walt Disney, Oprah Winfrey, and 19 Other Successful People Rebounded After Getting Fired." Business Insider, October 7, 2015, https://www.inc.com/business-insider/21-successful-people-who-rebounded-after-getting-fired.html

Gladwell, Malcolm. *Blink: The Power of Thinking without Thinking.* New York: Little, Brown and Company, 2007.

Glenn, Devon. "The History of Social Media from 1978-2012."

AdWeek, February 16, 2012, http://www.adweek.com/digital/the-history-of-social-media-from-1978-2012-infographic/

Gooden, Philip. *Skyscapers Hemlines and the Eddie Murphy Rule: Life's Hidden Laws Rules & Theories*. New York: Bloomsbury Publishing, 2015.

Gowin, Joshua. "Why Sharing Stories Brings People Together." *Psychology Today,* June 6, 2011.

Green, Chaz. "The History of Search Engines & Google Domination." Kazooky Media, June 22, 2015, http://www.kazooky.com/the-history-of-search-engines-google-domination/

Greene, Robert. *The 33 Strategies of War*. London: Penguin Books, 2006.

Hadhazy, Adam. "Life's Extremes: Early Birds vs. Night Owls." Live Science, October 2, 2011. https://www.livescience.com/16334-night-owls-early-birds-sleep-cycles.html

Harmon, Ken. "What Makes You Happy?" Speech, Kennesaw, GA, 2015.

Hasson, Uri. "This is your brain on communication." TED Talk. 14:52, February 18, 2016, https://www.ted.com/talks/uri_hasson_this_is_your_brain_on_communication

Henry David Thoreau Quotes. "BrainyQuote.com." Xplore Inc, https://www.brainyquote.com/authors/henry_david_thoreau (accessed March 15, 2018).

Hill, Idalia. "PwC Commits $320 Million to Help Improve Technology & Financial Capability of More Than 10 Million Students." PwC, New York, March 30, 2017, https://www.pwc.com/us/en/press-releases/2017/access-your-potential-aims-to-help-10-million-students.html

Hill, Napoleon. *Think and Grow Rich.* Pennsylvania: Sound Wisdom, 2016.

Hindle, Tim. *The Economist Guide to Management Ideas and Gurus.* New York: Bloomberg Press, 2008.

Hodin, Rachel. "35 Famous People Who Were Painfully Rejected Before Making It Big." Thought Catalog, October 14, 2013, https://thoughtcatalog.com/rachel-hodin/2013/10/35-famous-people-who-were-painfully-rejected-before-making-it-big/

Holodny, Elena. "Everyone forgets the most important thing about the 1987 Black Monday stock market crash." Business Insider, October 19, 2017, http://www.businessinsider.com/1987-black-monday-stock-market-crash-most-important-lesson-2017-10

Horne, J.A. and O. Ostberg. "A self-assessment questionnaire to determine morningness-eveningness in human circadian rhythms." *International Journal of Chronobiology*, no. 4 (1976): 97-100.

Howell, Thomas. "New Sonnets and Pretty Pamphlets." Historically Speaking, January 19, 2011, https://idiomation.wordpress.com/tag/new-sonnets-and-pretty-pamphlets/

Jaffe, Eric. "Morning People vs. Night Owls: 9 Insights Backed By Science." Fast Company, May 19, 2015. https://www.fastcodesign.com/3046391/morning-people-vs-night-people-9-insights-backed-by-science

Janis, Irving L. *Victims of Groupthink: A psychological study of foreign-policy decisions and fiascoes.* New York: Houghton Mifflin, 1972.

Jefferson, Thomas, Abigail Adams, and John Adams. *The Adams-Jefferson Letters: The Complete Correspondence between Thomas Jefferson and Abigail and John Adam*, ed. Lester J. Cappon. Chapel Hill: University of North Carolina Press, 1988.

Kanazawa, Satoshi. "Why Night Owls Are More Intelligent Than Morning Larks." Psychology Today, May 9, 2010.

Kashdan, Todd. *Curious?* New York: William Morrow, 2009.

Keller, Christian B. and Ethan S. Rafuse. "The Civil War Battlefield Staff Ride in the Twenty-first Century." *Civil War History* 62, no.2 (June 2016): 201-213.

Konnikova, Maria. "The Struggles of a Psychologist Studying Self-Control." *The New Yorker*, October 9, 2014.

Levine, Moe. "The Whole Man." Trebidi Tales. June 2016, https://tribeditales.wordpress.com/2016/06/19/whole-man-theory

Livingston, Ron. *Office Space*. DVD. Directed by Mike Judge. Los Angeles: Twentieth Century Fox, 1999.

Loewenstein, George. "The Psychology of Curiosity: A Review and Reinterpretation." *Semantics Scholar American Psychological Association*, 1994, Vol. 116, No.1, 75-98.

Looper, Benjamin. Southeast Restoration. "Who is Southeast Restoration?" 2017, https://southeastrestoration.com/about-us/

Loudenback, Tanza. "Spanx founder Sara Blakely learned an important lesson about failure from her dad—now she's passing it on to her 4 kids." Business Insider, October 14, 2016, http://www.businessinsider.com/spanx-founder-sara-blakely-redefine-failure-2016-10

Martin, Gary. "The meaning and origin of the expression: Curiosity killed the cat." The Phrase Finder, https://www.phrases.org.uk/meanings/curiosity-killed-the-cat.html (accessed on March 17, 2018).

Matson, Jack V. *The art of innovation: Using intelligent fast failure.* University Park: Pennsylvania State University, 1991.

McGonigal, Kelly. *The Willpower Instinct.* London: The Penguin Group, 2012.

McGrath, Rita. "Transient Advantage." *Harvard Business Review,* June 2013.

Naughton, John. "Steve Jobs: Stanford commencement address, June 2005." The Guardian, October 8, 2011, https://www.theguardian.com/technology/2011/oct/09/steve-jobs-stanford-commencement-address

Newman, Kira M. "Four Reasons to Cultivate Patience." Greater Good, April 4, 2016. https://greatergood.berkeley.edu/article/item/four_reasons_to_cultivate_patience

Nielsen. "Why Collaboration Leads to Higher-Impact Innovations." Nielsen Report, December 01, 2015, http://www.nielsen.com/us/en/insights/news/2015/why-collaboration-leads-to-higher-impact-innovations.html

Nietzsche, Friedrich. *Human, All-Too-Human: Parts One and Two.* New York: Dover Publications, 2006.

Orloff, Judith. *Emotional Freedom: Liberate Yourself from Negative Emotions and Transform Your Life.* New York: Harmony Books, 2009.

Penniman, Little Richard. *Poor Dog.* California: Columbia Studios, 1966.

Perrin, Andrew. "Book Reading 2016." Pew Research Center, September 1, 2016, http://www.pewinternet.org/2016/09/01/book-reading-2016/

Petroski, Henry. *To Engineer is Human: The Role of Failure in Successful Design.* New York: Vintage Publications, 1992.

Pope, Alexander. "An Essay on Criticism." Poetry Foundation, October 13, 2009, https://www.poetryfoundation.org/articles/69379/an-essay-on-criticism

Pressfield, Steven. *Do the Work*. New York: Black Irish Books, 2015.

Ray, John. *A Complete Collection of English Proverbs*. London: Forgotten Books, 2017.

Reed, Brad. "A Palm Technology Timeline." PC World, April 30, 2010, https://www.pcworld.com/article/195350/a_palm_technology_timeline.html

Rhodes, Hugh. *The Boke of Nurture for Men Servants and Children*. Charleston: Nabu Press, 2012.

Rigby, Butch. "History Laugh-O-Gram." Thank You Walt Disney, Inc., https://thankyouwaltdisney.org/history/ (accessed March 17, 2018).

Rolfe, Edwin and Lester Fuller. *Murder in the Glass Room*. New York: Bantam Books, 1948.

Rubin, Harriet. "C.E.O. Libraries Reveal Keys to Succes." New York Times, July 21, 2007.

Sampson, Curt. *A Vision, Not a Blueprint—Weldon Wyatt and Sage Valley*. Curt Sampson, 2007.

Sapadin, Linda. *Master Your Fears: How to Triumph Over Your Worries and Get on with Your Life*. Hoboken: John Wiley & Sons, 2004.

Schnitker, Sarah. "An Examination of Patience and Well-being." *The Journal of Positive Psychology* 7, no. 4 (June 26, 2012): 263-280.

Selin, Shannon. "Bonaparte the Bookworm—Napoleon was an avid reader; so what were his favourite books?" Military History Now, April 15, 2015, http://militaryhistorynow.com/2015/04/15/bonaparte

Shearer, Harry. *The Simpsons Movie.* DVD, Directed by David Silverman. Los Angeles: Twentieth Century Fox, 2007.

Shepard, Alan, Deke Slayton, Jay Barbree and Howard Benedict. *Moon Shot: The Inside Story of America's Race to the Moon.* Nashville: Turner Publishing, 1994.

Siebold, Steve. *How Rich People Think.* Naperville: Simple Truths, 2014.

Sitkin, Slim B. *Learning Through Failure: The Strategy of Small Losses.* Austin: University of Texas, 1990.

Sloane, Paul. *Lateral Thinking Puzzlers.* New York: Puzzle Wright Press, 2016.

Smith, Adam. *The Wealth of Nations.* London: W. Strahan and T. Cadell, 1776.

Smith, Jacquelyn. "The Insane Work Ethic of Mark Cuban, Jeff Bezos, and 14 Other Powerful Leaders." Business Insider, April 8, 2016, https://www.inc.com/business-insider/work-ethic-of-super-successful-people.html

Stansberry, Glen. "How to Become a Modern Day Renaissance Man (or Woman)." Gentlemint, April 14, 2017, http://blog.gentlemint.com/2017/jan/18/renaissance-man/

Stephen, Bijan. "You Won't Believe How Little Americans Read." *Time,* June 22, 2014.

Sugar, Rachel. "15 People Who Prove You Don't Have to Wake up Early to be Successful." Business Insider, July 12, 2015. http://www.businessinsider.com/successful-people-who-wake-up-late-2015-7

Tasler, Nick. "Make Good Decisions Faster." *Harvard Business Review*, July 05, 2013.

Ted Turner Quotes. "BrainyQuote.com." Xplore Inc, https://www.brainyquote.com/authors/ted_turner (accessed March 15, 2018).

Tellis, Gerard J. and Peter N. Golder. *Will and Vision: How Latecomers Grow to Dominate Markets*. New York: McGraw-Hill, 2001.

Treasurer, Bill. *Courage Goes to Work: How to Build Backbones, Boost Performance, and Get Results*. Oakland: Berrett-Koehler Publishers, 2008.

Twitchell, James B. *Branded Nation: The Marketing of Megachurch, College Inc., and Museumworld*. New York: Simon & Schuster, 2004.

Villines, Zawn. "The Psychology of Risk-Taking." Good Therapy.org, May 7, 2013, https://www.goodtherapy.org/blog/risks-adrenaline-benefits-neuroticism-0418137

Waber, Ben, Jennifer Magnolfi and Greg Lindsay. "Workspaces That Move People." *Harvard Business Review*, October 2014.

Ward, Marguerite. "Warren Buffet's reading routine could make you smarter, science suggests." CNBC, November 16, 2016, https://www.cnbc.com/2016/11/16/warren-buffetts-reading-routine-could-make-you-smarter-suggests-science.html

Watanabe, Takeo, Y. Yotsumoto, LH Chang, R. Ni, R. Pierce, G.J. Andersen, Y. Sasaki. "White Matter in the Older Brain is More Plastic Than in the Younger Brain." Nature Communications, November 19, 2014, https://www.ncbi.nlm.nih.gov/pubmed/25407566

Weissmann, Jordan. "The Decline of the American Book Lover." *The Atlantic*, January 21, 2014.